Plastic Canvas Stitch Dictionary

You won't believe how much fun you can have with plastic canvas! With this handy reference to guide you, you'll breeze through all kinds of plain and fancy stitches, joining methods, and other techniques. This book teaches everything you need to know about plastic canvas, and it's as easy to use as a dictionary! More than 100 stitches are arranged alphabetically and accompanied by color photographs, clear diagrams, and simple-to-follow instructions. So you can practice your new skills right away, we also present five eye-catching projects that feature a variety of the stitches. You'll keep this indispensable aid in your stitching basket for years to come!

TABLE OF CONTENTS

PAGE

Stitch Dictionary..2

Sample Projects...28
   Tissue Box Cover 28
   Doorstop 30
   Bellpull Sampler 32
   Eyeglass Case 35
   Coasters 36

Stitch Specifics 38
   Types of Stitches 38
   Compensating Stitches 38
   Stitch Placement 38

Plastic Canvas Pointers..38
   Selecting Canvas 38
   Selecting Needles 38
   Selecting Yarn 39
   Working With Plastic Canvas 40
   Stitching the Design 40
   Joining Pieces 40
   Washing Your Project 40

Stitch Index..41

Copyright © 1997 by Leisure Arts, Inc., 104 Champs Blvd., STE 100, Maumelle, AR 72113-6738, www.leisurearts.com.
All rights reserved. This publication is protected under federal copyright laws. Reproduction or distribution of this publication or any other Leisure Arts publication, including publications which are out of print, is prohibited unless specifically authorized. This includes, but is not limited to, any form of reproduction or distribution on or through the Internet, including posting, scanning or e-mail transmission.

STITCH DICTIONARY

When working any of these stitches, always bring threaded needle up at 1 (A or a) and go down at 2 (B or b) and follow sequence, unless otherwise noted.

 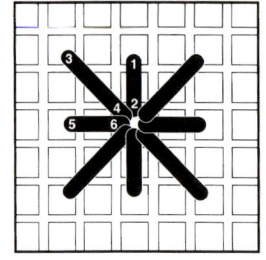

ALGERIAN EYE STITCH
This stitch forms a square over four threads of canvas. It consists of eight stitches worked in a counterclockwise fashion. Each stitch is worked from the outer edge into the same central hole.

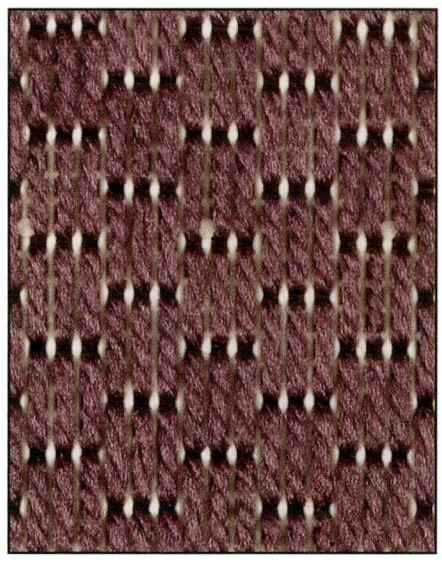 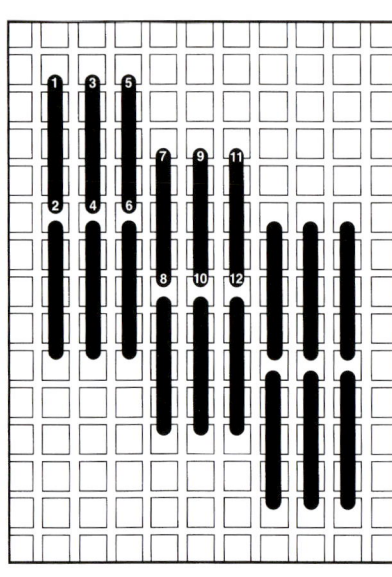

ALGERIAN FILLING STITCH
This stitch is made up of straight stitches that form a stair-step pattern. For added interest, multiple colors may be used.

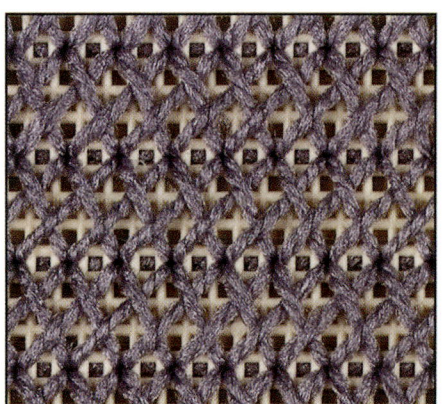 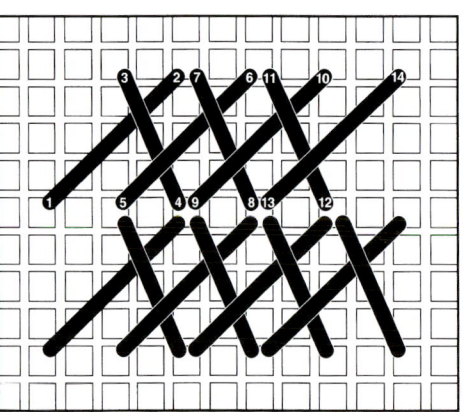

ALGERIAN PLAITED STITCH
This crossed stitch is always worked from left to right and creates a lacy pattern.

 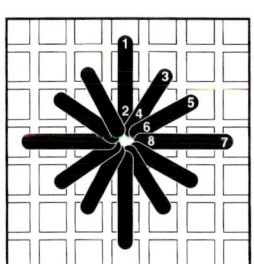

ALGERIAN STAR STITCH
This diamond pattern is a larger variation of the Algerian Eye Stitch, but it is worked in a clockwise manner. It consists of twelve stitches, each worked from the outer edge into the same central hole.

ALICIA LACE STITCH
This series of stitches forms a lacy pattern. It consists of simple rows of Tent and Reversed Tent Stitches.

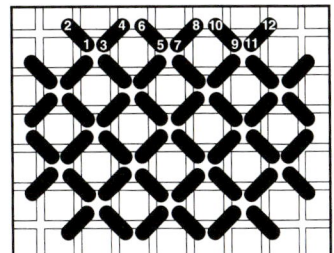 

ARROWHEAD STITCH
This stitch is composed of slanting stitches that form an arrowhead shape. A horizontal row of Backstitches is worked through the center of each arrowhead.

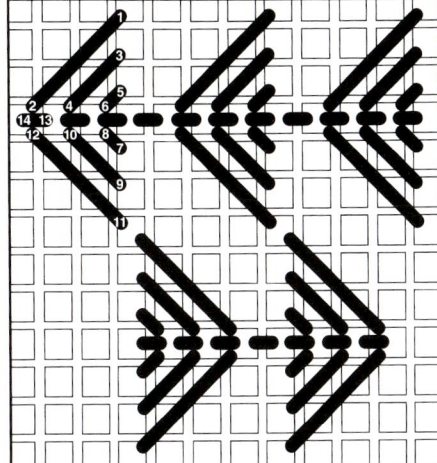 

BACKSTITCH — ACCENT/DETAIL
This stitch is worked over completed stitches to outline or define. Each stitch may be worked in any direction and over more than one thread.

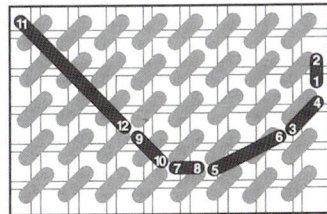 

BACKSTITCH — GENERAL COVERAGE
This small stitch is worked in a backward motion over one thread of canvas. It is usually used to cover small areas that require much detail.

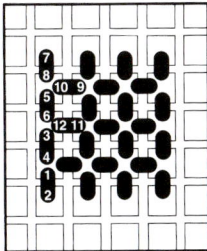 

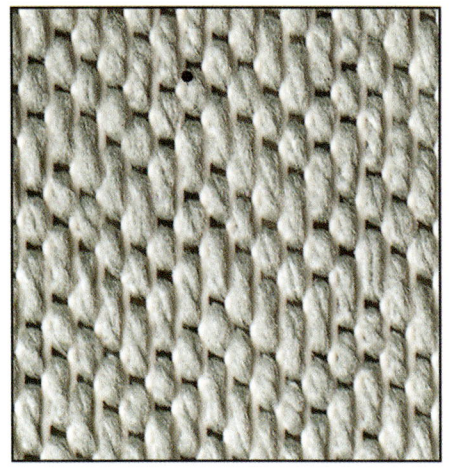 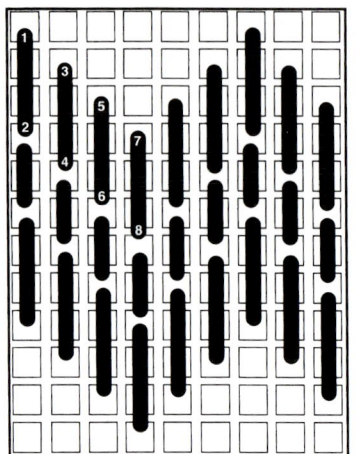

BARGELLO STITCH
This stitch is a repeated combination of vertical straight stitches that form a wave pattern. Bargello Stitch can be worked over any combination of threads.

 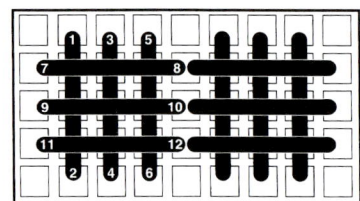

BARRED SQUARE STITCH
This stitch is composed of six straight stitches. The three horizontal stitches are worked on top of the three vertical stitches.

  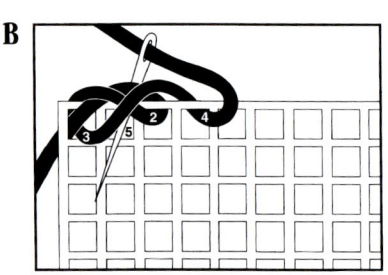 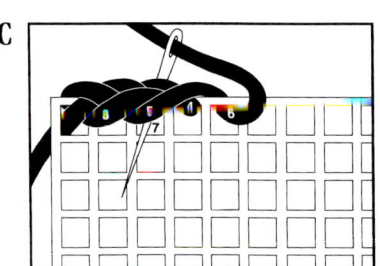

BRAIDED CROSS STITCH
This stitch covers the edge of the canvas or joins pieces of canvas. Begin by working stitches 1 through 3 (**A**). Starting with 4, proceed to work stitches in **B** and **C**, working forward over three threads and back over two. It may be necessary to work extra stitches at corners for better coverage.

4

BRICK STITCH — BASIC
This background stitch is worked in a step pattern that resembles brickwork.

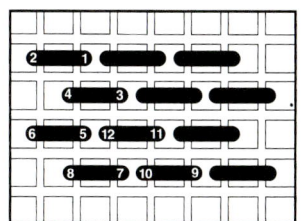 

BRICK STITCH — DOUBLE
This series of stitches is worked over four threads, forming staggering rows.

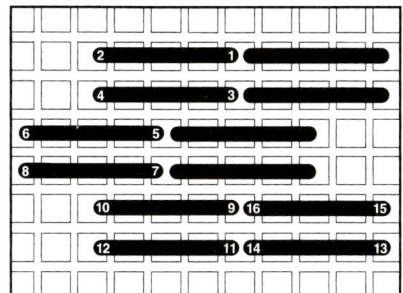 

BULLION KNOT
Bring needle up at 1 and go down at 2, leaving a loose loop on top of the canvas. The distance between 1 and 2 is the length of the knot. Come up at 1 again, but do not pull needle through to top of canvas. Wrap loop around needle several times, making first wrap close to canvas and remaining wraps very close together (**A**). The number of wraps will depend on the distance between 1 and 2 and the amount of curve desired in the finished stitch. Hold wraps in place with non-stitching fingers and pull needle and yarn through wraps (**B**), holding wraps until they must be released. Pull yarn until wraps lie on canvas; secure knot by going down at 2 (**C**). Use tip of needle to evenly distribute wraps if necessary. Several Bullion Knots can be worked together to form flower petals or leaves or a Bullion Rose.

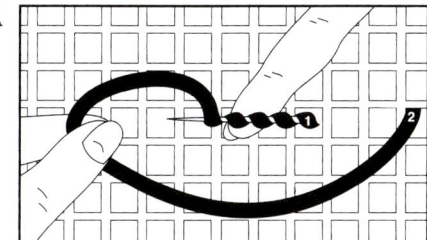
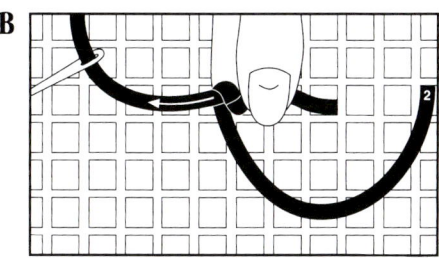

BYZANTINE STITCH — BASIC
A zigzag effect is created by the Byzantine Stitch. It is composed of slanting stitches worked in a diagonal pattern. The number of threads and intersections covered may vary.

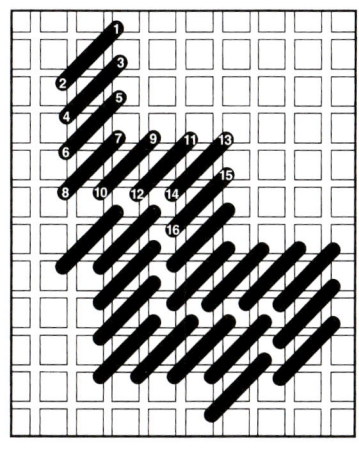 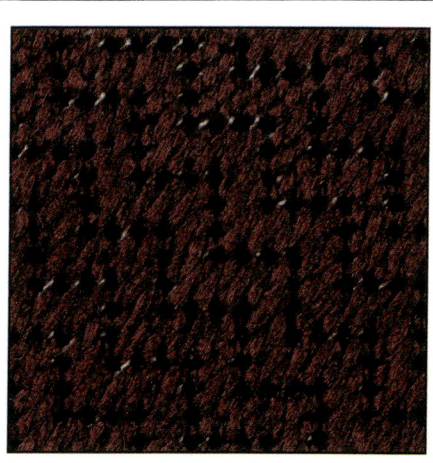

 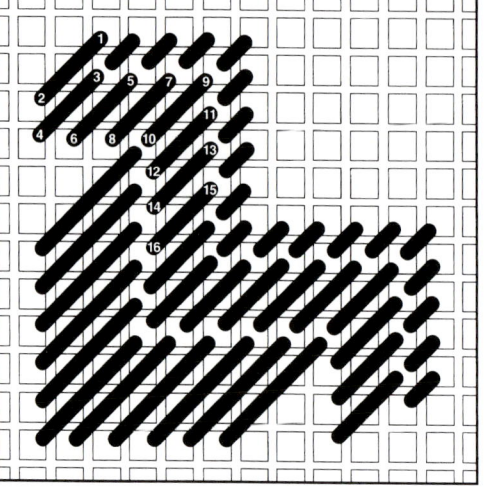

BYZANTINE STITCH — IRREGULAR
This stitch is composed of slanting stitches worked in a diagonal stair-step pattern. The number of threads and intersections covered will vary.

 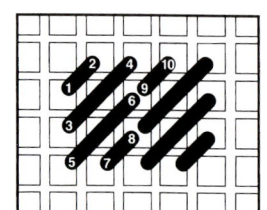

CASHMERE STITCH — BASIC
This small rectangle pattern is usually made up of four slanted stitches.

 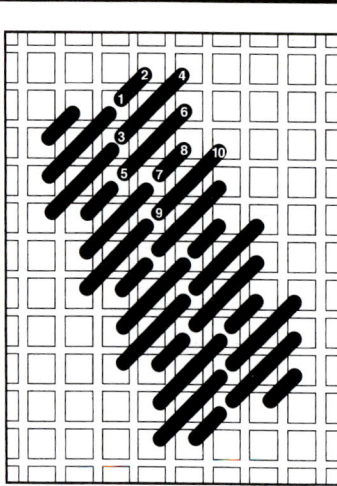

CASHMERE STITCH — CONDENSED
This stitch pattern is stitched diagonally rather than worked in straight rows.

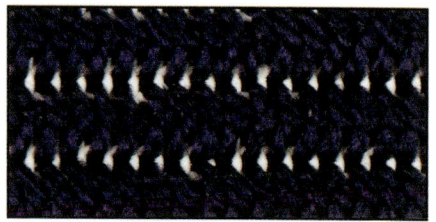 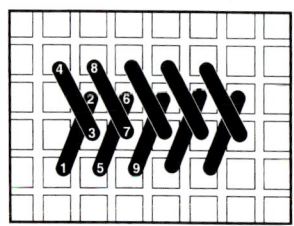

CHEVRON STITCH
This stitch pattern is composed of overlapping slanted stitches that are always worked from left to right.

CROSS STITCH — BASIC

This stitch is composed of two diagonal stitches. It is commonly worked over one intersection of threads. The direction of the top stitch may vary, but all stitches on a stitched piece should be made in the same direction. If covering a large area with Cross Stitches, it may be easier to work Tent Stitches all the way across and Reverse Tent Stitches all the way back, rather than crossing each stitch before going to the next.

CROSS STITCH — ALTERNATING

This pattern is made up of Basic Cross Stitches worked over one thread and Long-Legged Cross Stitches worked over three horizontal threads.

CROSS STITCH — BOUND

This decorative stitch is worked over four threads and forms a bold cross.

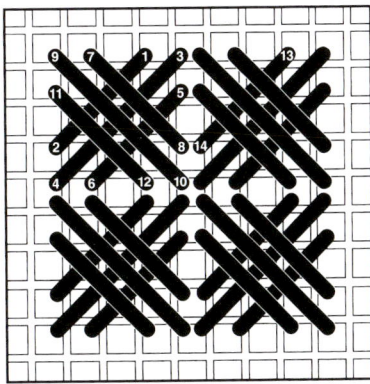

CROSS STITCH — DIAGONAL UPRIGHT

This stitch is composed of interlocking stitches that create a woven diagonal effect. Begin working each diagonal row from the left.

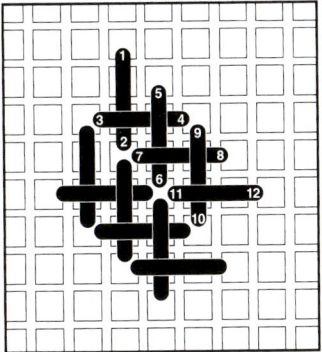

CROSS STITCH — DOUBLE
This stitch has a star shape. Each stitch is completed before starting the next one. The direction of the top stitch may vary, but all stitches on a stitched piece should be made in the same direction. This stitch has an alternating diamond effect when used as a general coverage stitch. When used to cover an area of canvas, this stitch is worked over four horizontal and four vertical threads. When used as an accent stitch over a previously stitched background, it may be worked over any even number of threads.

 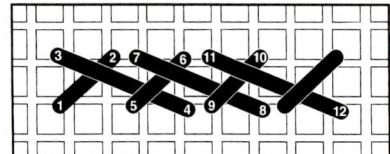

CROSS STITCH — IRREGULAR LONG-LEGGED
This is a series of stitches in which the long leg of one cross connects with the next to create a woven appearance. Always work this stitch from left to right.

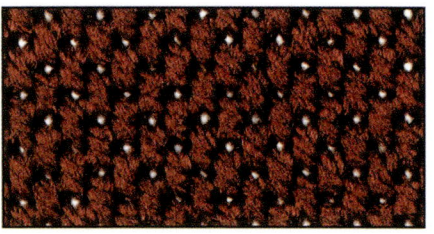 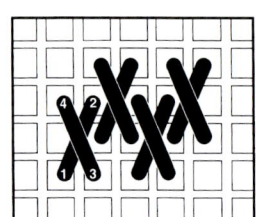

CROSS STITCH — LONG-LEGGED
This stitch is composed of two stitches. These stitches are nested together to cover the canvas. The direction of the top stitch may vary, but all stitches on a stitched piece should be made in the same direction.

CROSS STITCH — SMYRNA
This stitch is worked over two vertical and two horizontal threads. Each stitch is worked completely before going on to the next. The direction of the top stitch may vary, but all stitches on a stitched piece should be made in the same direction.

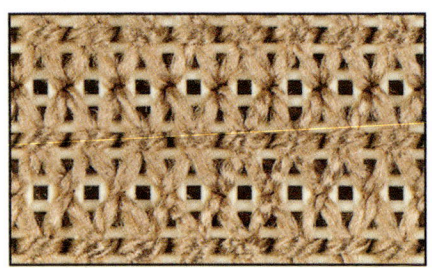 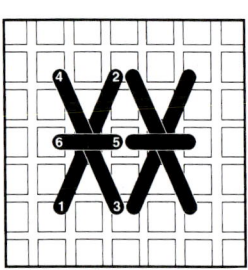

CROSS STITCH — TIED
Each stitch is worked completely before going on to the next and may be worked over any number of threads.

CROSS STITCH — TIED DOUBLE

This stitch is worked in three steps. It is often worked with three colors. With first color, work large Cross Stitches over four threads (**A**). Then, with second color, work an Upright Cross Stitch between large Cross Stitches (**B**). With third color, work Upright Cross Stitches over intersections of large crosses and where large Cross Stitches meet (**B**).

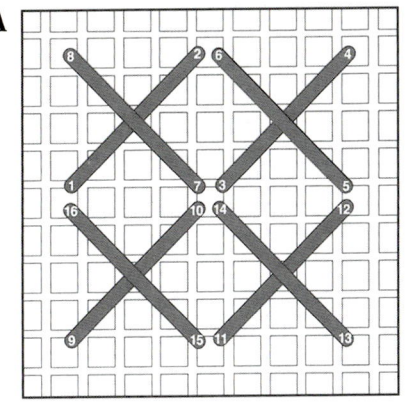

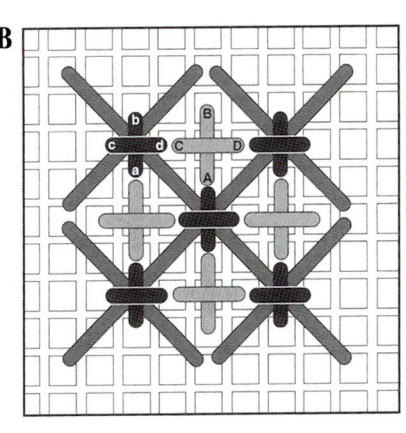

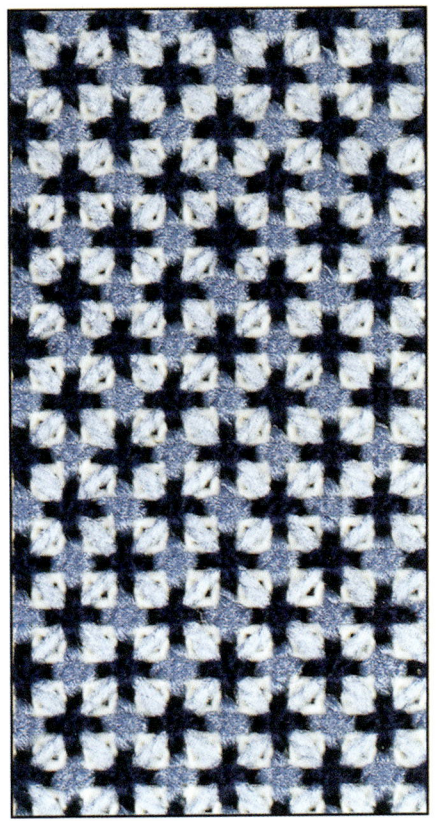

CROSS STITCH — TRIPLE

This square stitch is worked over three horizontal and three vertical threads. Each stitch is worked completely before going on to the next. The direction of the top stitch may vary, but all stitches on a stitched piece should be made in the same direction.

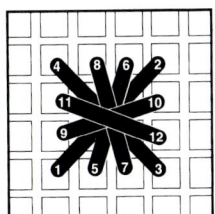

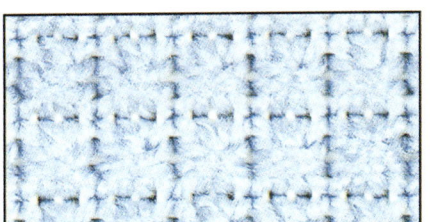

CROSS STITCH — UPRIGHT

One vertical and one horizontal stitch make up this stitch. Each stitch is worked completely before going on to the next. The direction of the top stitch may vary, but all stitches on a stitched piece should be made in the same direction.

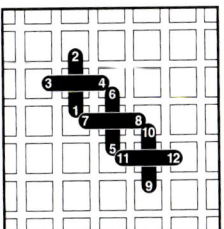

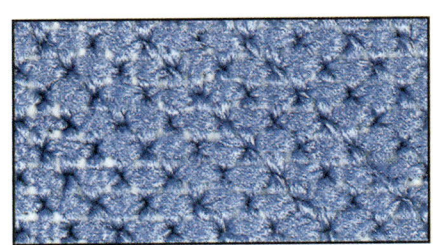

CROSS STITCH — WOUND

This stitch has a smooth, circular appearance. Work two horizontal and two vertical stitches into the same central hole (**A**). Bring needle up at 1 and wrap yarn in a circular fashion under all horizontal and vertical stitches. Making sure the yarn lies flat, continue wrapping yarn to fill stitches. Bring needle down at 4 and secure yarn on wrong side of canvas (**B**). The size of the stitch may vary.

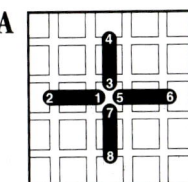

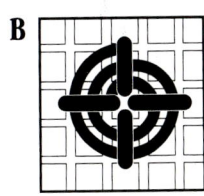

 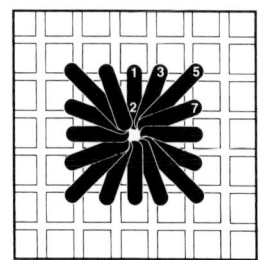

EYELET STITCH
This stitch forms a square over four threads of canvas. It consists of 16 stitches worked in a clockwise fashion. Each stitch is worked from the outer edge into the same central hole.

 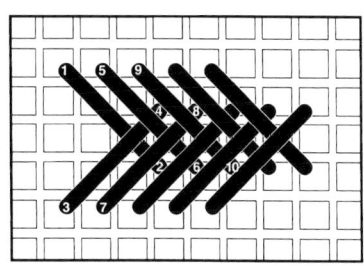

FERN STITCH — BASIC
These slanted stitches are worked in an overlapping pattern that has a braided look.

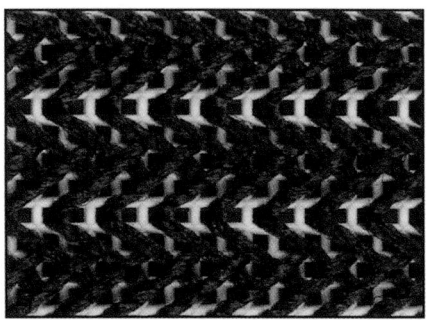 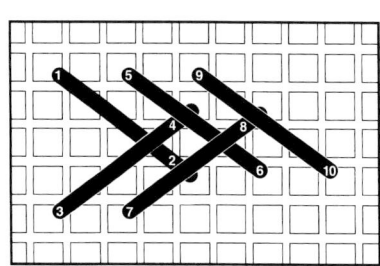

FERN STITCH — OPEN VARIATION
Leaving an unworked hole between slanted stitches gives this variation a loosely braided look.

 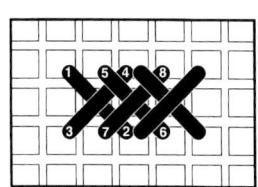

FERN STITCH — VARIATION
This stitch pattern is actually a row of large, overlapping Cross Stitches.

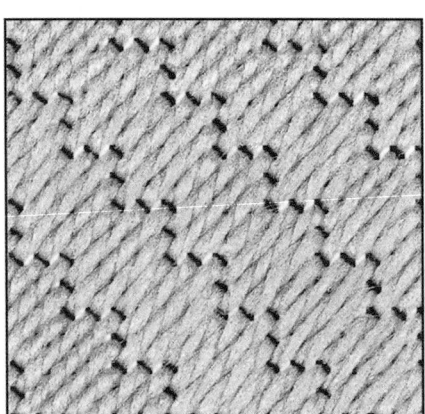 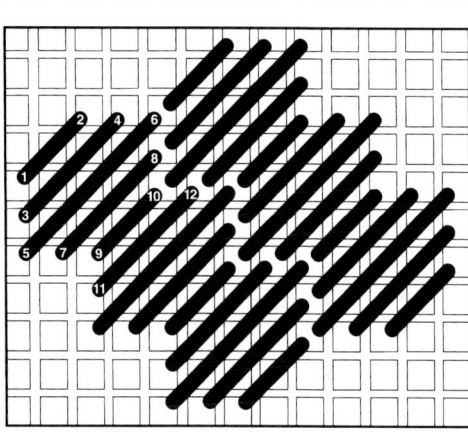

FLAT STITCH
This series of slanted stitches, also called Condensed Stitch, is worked in diagonal rows and has a slightly wavy appearance.

FLORENTINE STITCH — BASIC
This series of straight stitches has a wave-like appearance when worked in multiple colors. The size of the waves may vary.

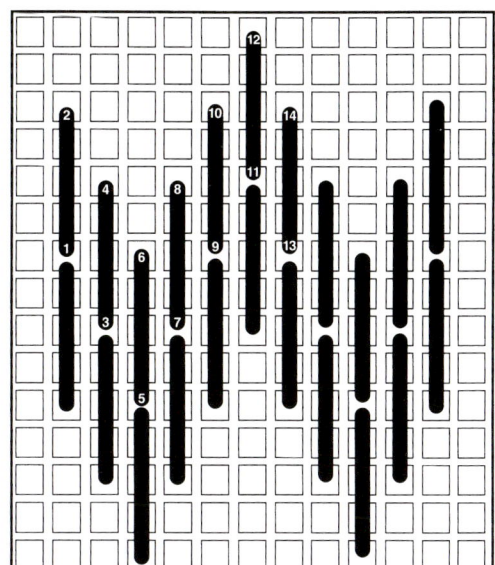 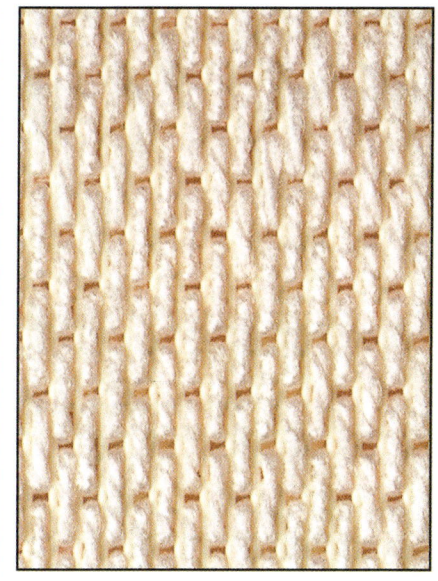

FLORENTINE STITCH — VARIATION
This series of straight stitches creates a diamond pattern. Varying the number of stitches in each part of the pattern will alter the shape of the diamonds. The size of the diamonds may vary.

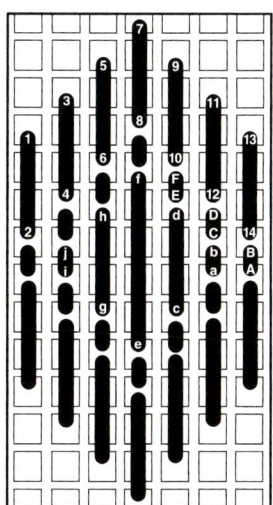 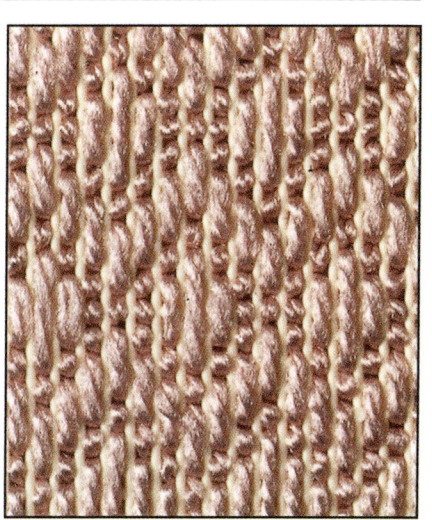

FRENCH KNOT — BASIC
Bring needle up through hole. Wrap yarn around needle once and insert in same or adjacent hole. Tighten knot as close to canvas as possible as you pull the needle and yarn back through canvas. Two pieces of canvas may also be joined by simply working a French Knot through both pieces.

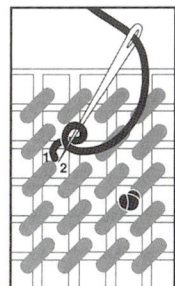 

FRENCH KNOT — DOUBLE
Bring needle up through hole. Wrap yarn around needle twice and insert needle in same or adjacent hole. Tighten knot as close to canvas as possible as you pull the needle and yarn back through canvas. To join two pieces of canvas, work a Double French Knot through both pieces.

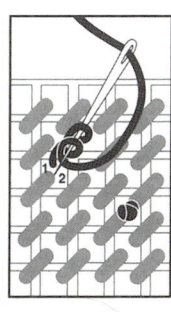 

 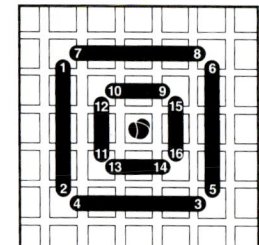

FRENCH KNOT — FRAMED
This stitch is composed of a French Knot surrounded by Straight Gobelin Stitches that form squares.

 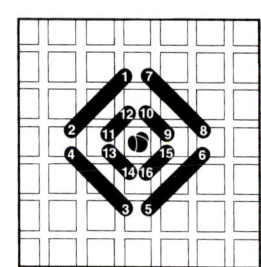

FRENCH KNOT — DIAGONAL FRAMED
This stitch is composed of a French Knot surrounded by Slanted Gobelin Stitches that form diagonal squares.

 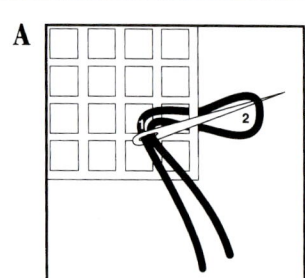

FRINGE STITCH — ON EDGE OF CANVAS
Fold a length of yarn in half. Thread needle with loose ends of yarn. Bring needle up at 1, leaving a 1" loop on the back of the canvas. Bring needle around the edge of canvas and through loop (**A**). Pull to tighten loop (**B**). Trim Fringe to desired length. A dot of glue on back of Fringe will help keep stitch in place.

 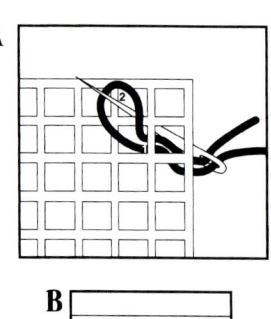

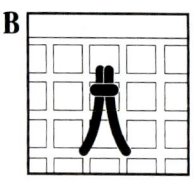

FRINGE STITCH — ON CANVAS INTERIOR
Fold a length of yarn in half. Thread needle with loose ends of yarn. Take needle down at 1, leaving a 1" loop on front of the canvas. Bring needle up at 2 in adjacent hole and through loop (**A**). Pull to tighten loop (**B**). Trim Fringe to desired length. A dot of glue on back of Fringe will help keep stitch in place.

GOBELIN STITCH — SLANTING

This stitch covers more than one intersection of threads and may slant in either direction. It may be worked in rows, either horizontally or vertically. The number of intersections may vary.

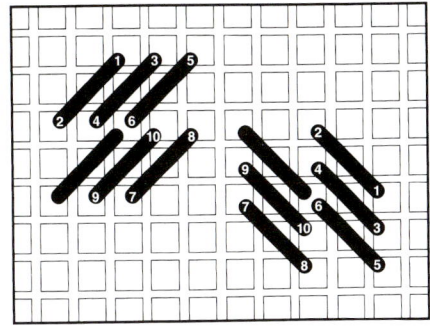 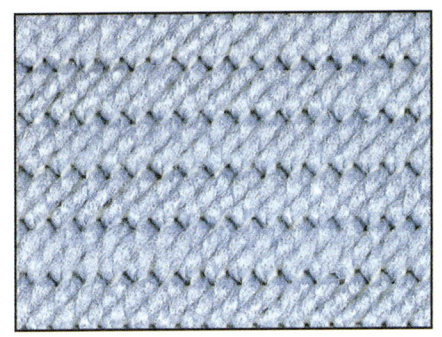

GOBELIN STITCH — STRAIGHT

This basic straight stitch is worked over two or more threads. Stitches may be worked in rows, either horizontally or vertically. The number of threads may vary.

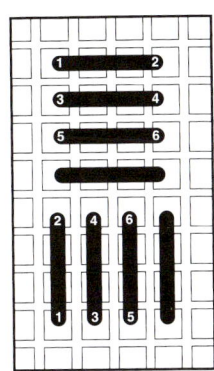 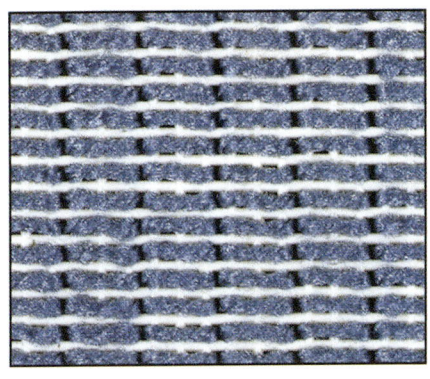

GOBELIN — ENCROACHING

This stitch creates a closely woven effect. Each stitch is worked over four horizontal threads and diagonally over one vertical thread. Each row overlaps the previous row by one thread.

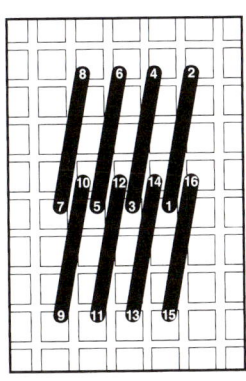 

GOBELIN STITCH — PADDED

This stitch is composed of one long straight Gobelin Stitch covered with shorter, straight or slanted Gobelin Stitches.

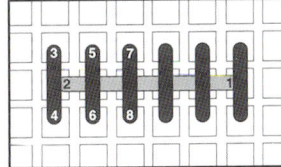 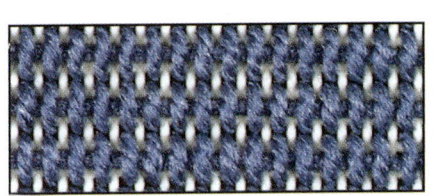

GREEK STITCH

This stitch has a braid-like appearance. Rows are worked in a back and forth manner.

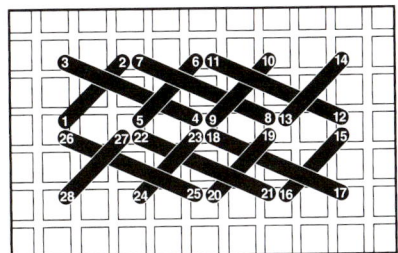 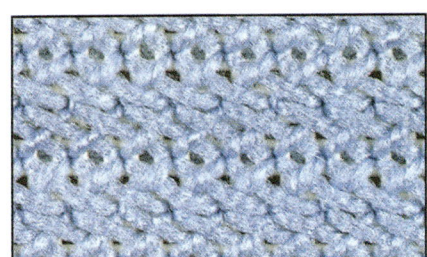

 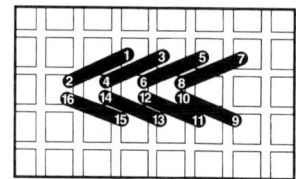

HERRINGBONE STITCH — BASIC
Alternating rows of slanted stitches form this pattern. Each stitch is worked over one horizontal thread and two vertical threads.

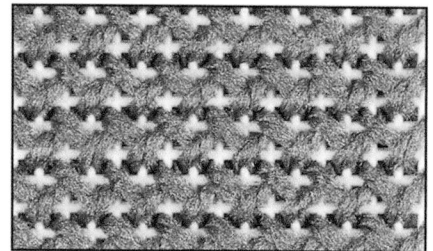 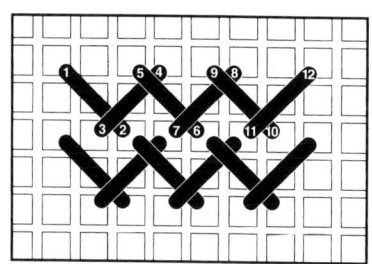

HERRINGBONE STITCH — CROSSED
This stitch has a woven appearance. Always work from left to right across the canvas.

 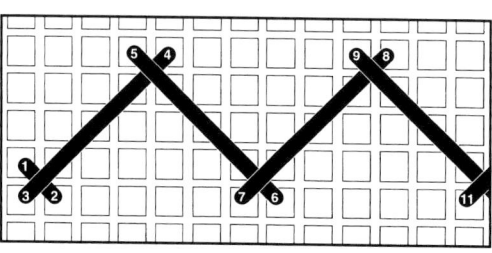

HERRINGBONE STITCH — SIX TRIP
Six rows of stitches form this pattern. Work each row from left to right. This pattern is sometimes worked with as many as six different colors or shades.

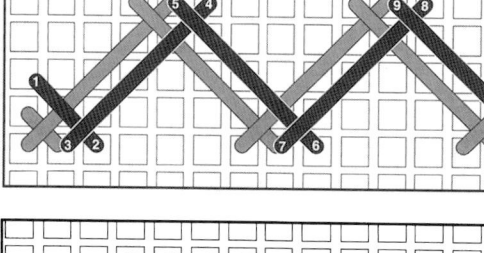

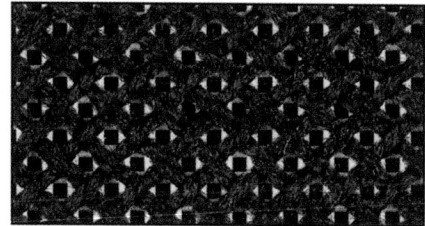 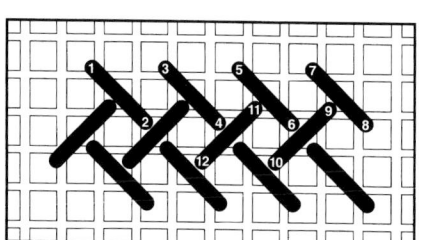

HERRINGBONE STITCH — SQUARE
This pattern has an open-weave appearance.

HORIZONTAL FLY STITCH
This stitch is composed of two rows of slanted stitches with a horizontal row of Backstitches worked between the rows of slanted stitches.

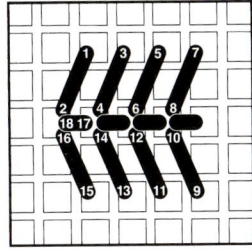 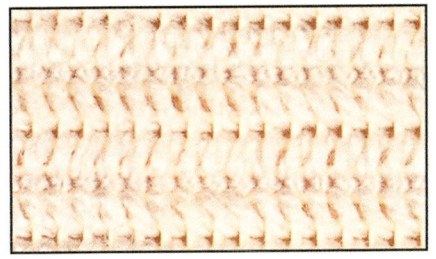

HUNGARIAN STITCH — BASIC
Rows of straight stitches form this pattern. Each row is set into the preceding row.

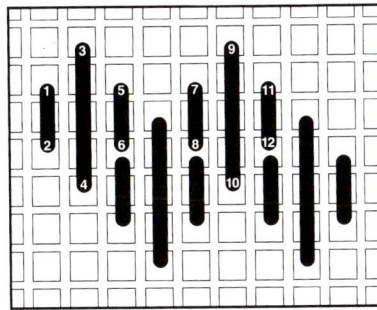 

HUNGARIAN STITCH — DIAMOND
This is a larger variation of the Basic Hungarian Stitch. Rows of straight stitches are worked over horizontal threads.

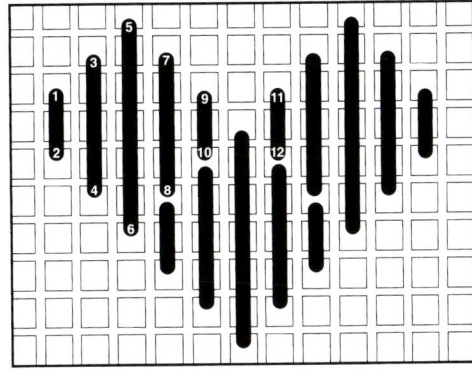 

HUNGARIAN STITCH — DIAMOND VARIATION
Horizontal and vertical straight stitches are combined to form this large diamond pattern.

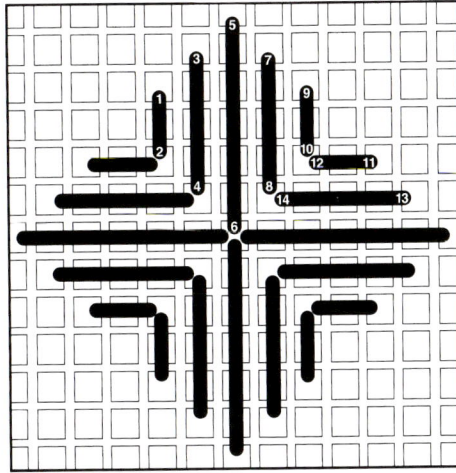 

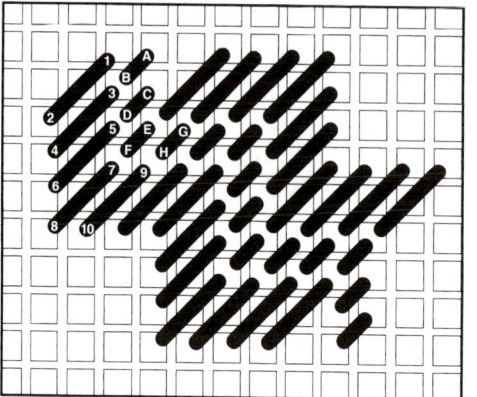

JACQUARD STITCH
Slanted stitches worked over two intersections alternate with Tent Stitches to create this stitch.

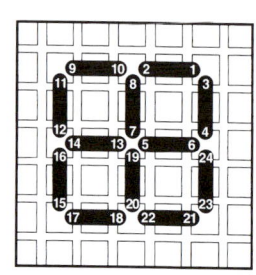

LACE STITCH
This stitch pattern forms small, open squares.

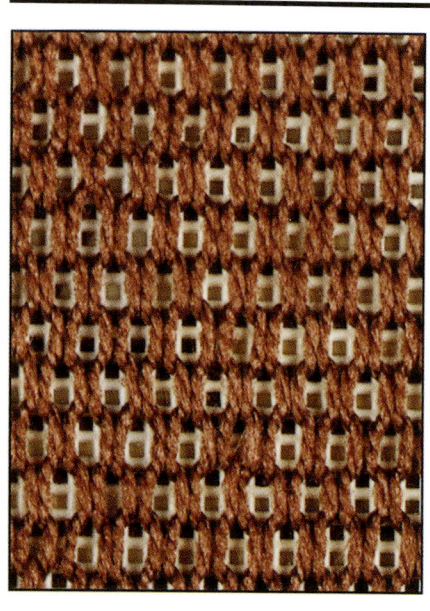
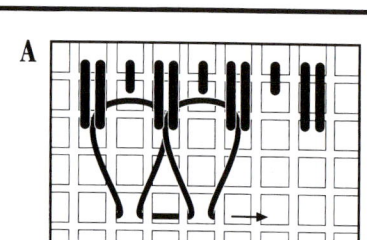
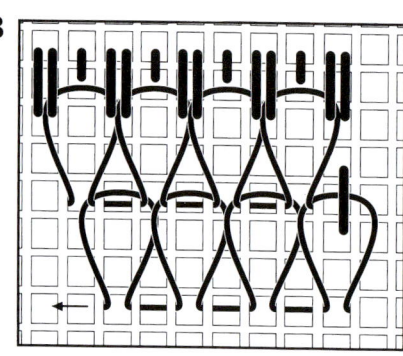

LACED CHAIN STITCH
This pattern has a knitted look. The first row of loops is formed by weaving yarn under the straight stitches and through the canvas (**A**). Continue weaving under previous row of loops and through canvas (**B**). Always work in direction of the arrows.

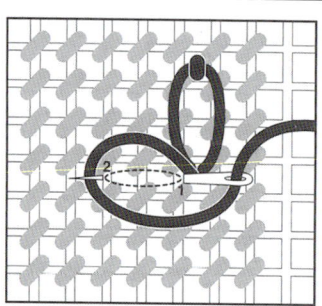

LAZY DAISY STITCH
This loop stitch can be used for flower petals or leaves. Bring needle up at 1. Insert needle in the same hole, leaving a loop on top of canvas. Bring needle up at 2 and through the loop. To secure loop, insert needle at 2 and gently pull yarn back through canvas until loop lies flat on the canvas.

LEAF STITCH — BASIC
Composed of nine straight and slanted stitches worked in a clockwise direction, this stitch may be worked vertically or horizontally. The length of the stitches may vary.

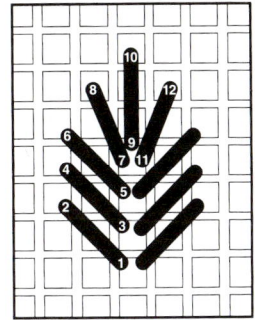 

LEAF STITCH — DIAGONAL
Work the eight straight Gobelin Stitches in a counterclockwise direction before adding the long, slanted Gobelin Stitch. The length of the stitches may vary.

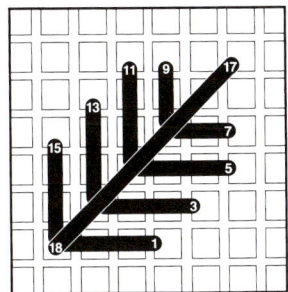 

LEVIATHAN STITCH — BASIC
This stitch is worked over four threads and is composed of four stitches, all crossing at the center.

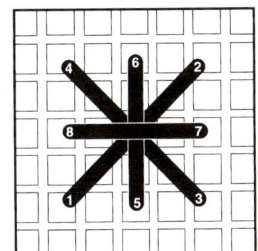 

LEVIATHAN STITCH — DOUBLE
This stitch is worked over four threads and is composed of eight stitches, all crossing at the center.

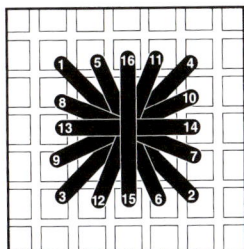 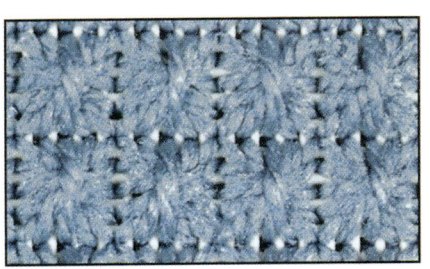

LEVIATHAN STITCH — DOUBLE VARIATION
This stitch gets its diamond shape by replacing the final horizontal and vertical stitches of the Double Leviathan Stitch with five small Upright Cross Stitches.

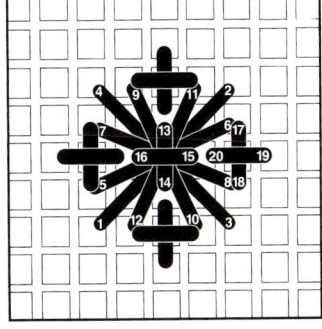 

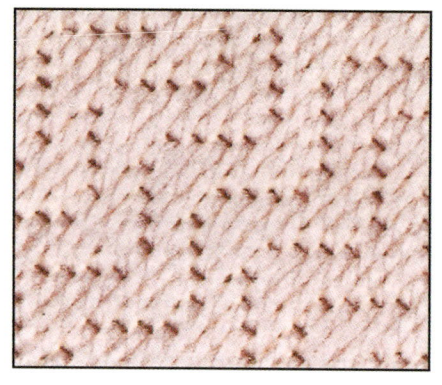 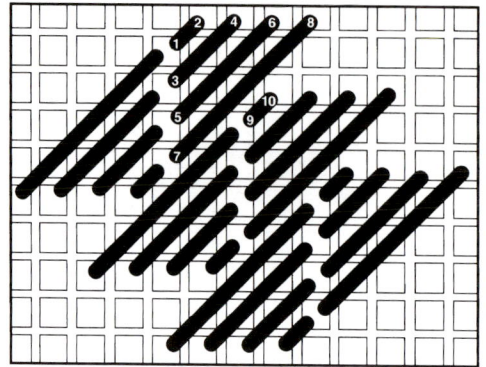

MILANESE STITCH
The Milanese is a series of triangular-shaped stitches. The diagonal rows are worked side by side to fill in background areas. The direction of the triangles alternates with each row.

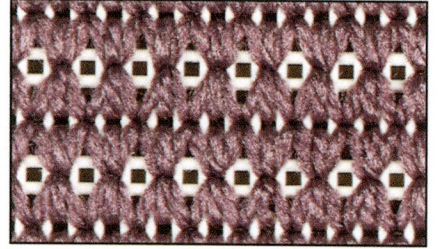 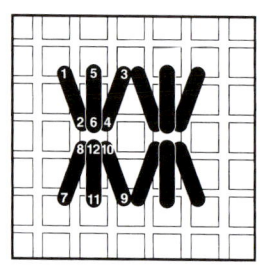

MOCK WHEAT STITCH
This stitch is composed of six Gobelin Stitches and looks similar to a bundle of wheat. All six stitches go down in the same center hole.

MOSAIC STITCH — BASIC
This three-stitch pattern forms small squares.

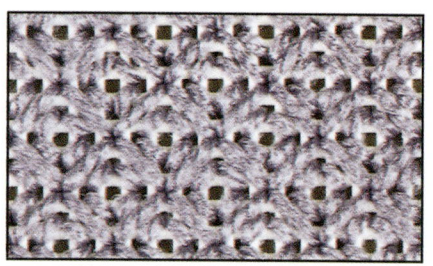 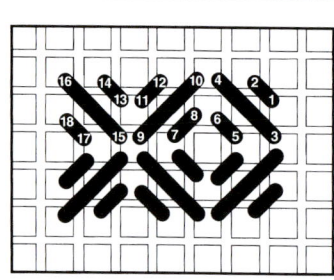

MOSAIC STITCH — ALTERNATING
This stitch is made by working Mosaic Stitches in alternating directions.

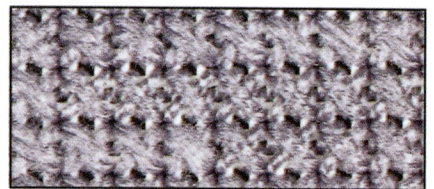 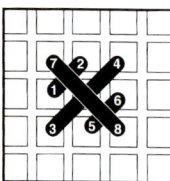

MOSAIC STITCH — CROSSED
This stitch starts with a Mosaic Stitch then adds a top stitch that crosses the Mosaic Stitch.

 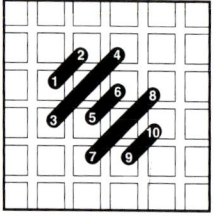

MOSAIC STITCH — DIAGONAL
A variation of the Mosaic Stitch, this stitch is worked in diagonal rows.

ORIENTAL STITCH
Diagonal rows of triangle-shaped stitches, stitched in opposite directions are combined to form this pattern. Fill in between the rows of triangles with rows of Gobelin Stitches.

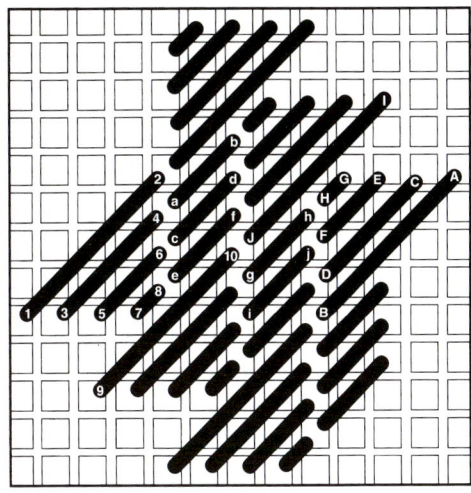 

OVERCAST STITCH — BASIC
This stitch covers the edge of the canvas or joins pieces of canvas. It may be necessary to go through the same hole more than once to get even coverage on the edge, especially at the corners.

OVERCAST STITCH — ALTERNATING
This two-colored stitch covers the edge of the canvas or joins pieces of canvas. With first color, work Overcast Stitches in every other hole. Then, with second color, work Overcast Stitches in remaining holes. It may be necessary to go through the same hole more than once to get even coverage on the edge, especially at the corners.

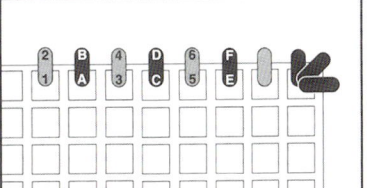 

PARISIAN STITCH — BASIC
This series of straight stitches worked in horizontal or vertical rows forms an interlocking pattern.

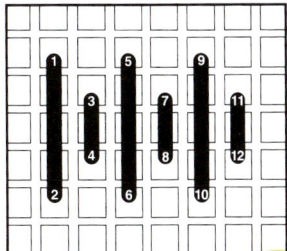 

PARISIAN STITCH — PADDED
This stitch is composed of one long straight stitch covered with a series of straight stitches worked in horizontal or vertical rows that form an interlocking pattern.

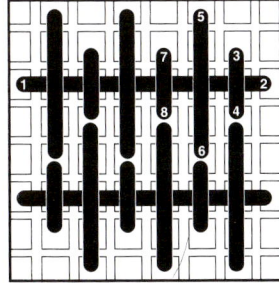 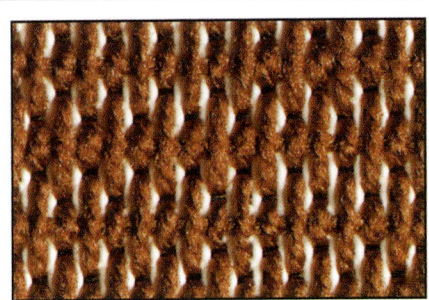

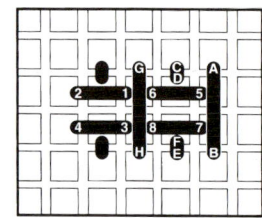

RAILROAD TRACKS STITCH
Work horizontal stitches first, then complete pattern with vertical stitches.

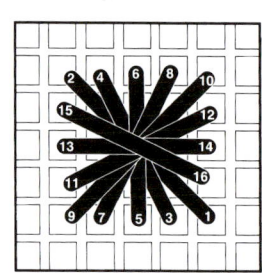

RHODES STITCH — BASIC
This square stitch looks similar to the Leviathan Stitch. Worked over any even number of threads, the stitches are worked in a clockwise direction.

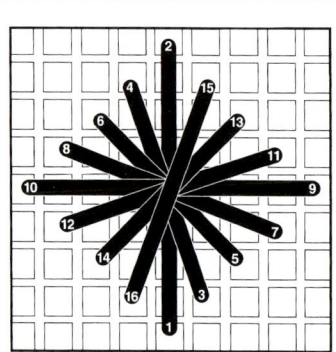

RHODES STITCH — DIAMOND
This diamond-shaped stitch is worked counterclockwise over eight threads.

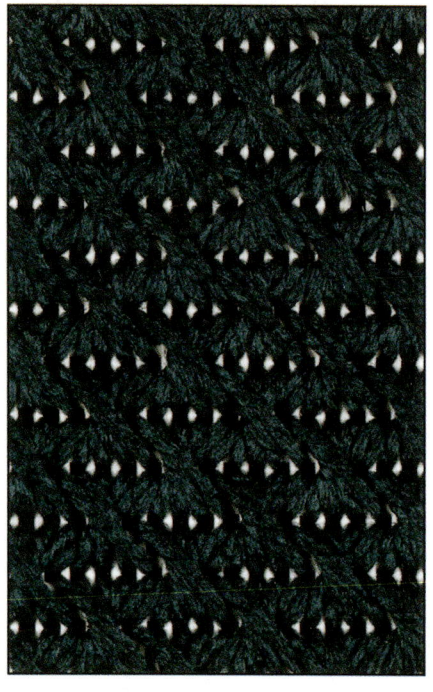
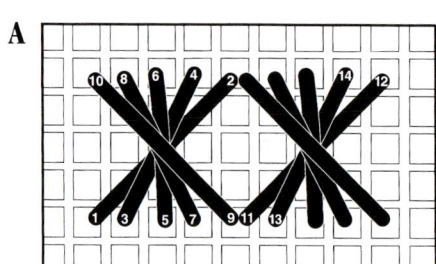
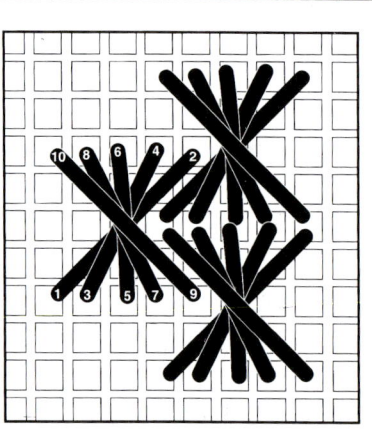

RHODES STITCH — HALF
This stitch may be worked in horizontal rows (**A**) or in an interlocking pattern (**B**).

RHODES STITCH — HEART

Work the stitches in a clockwise direction to form either the large (**A**) or small (**B**) variation of this stitch.

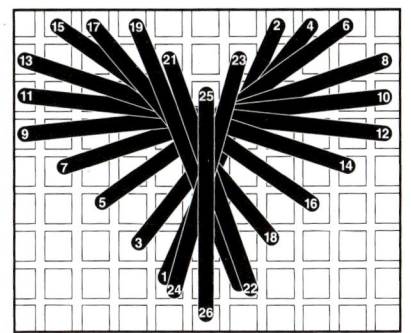
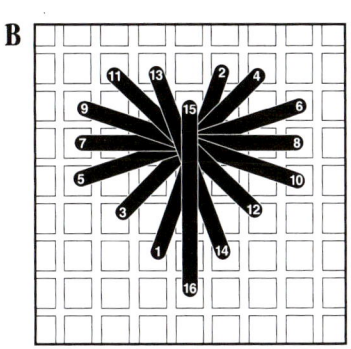
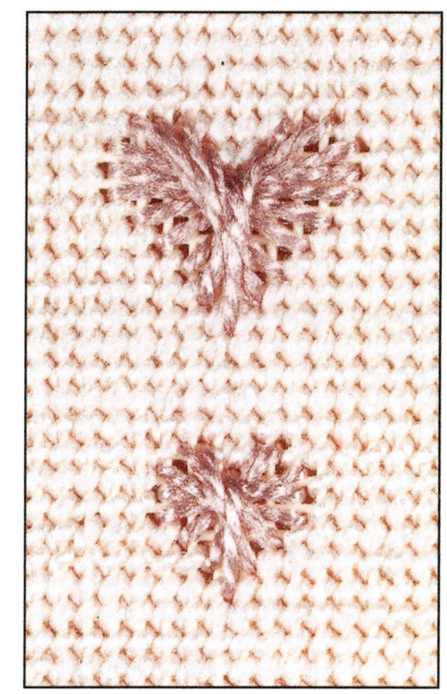

RHODES STITCH — OCTAGON

This heavy stitch is worked in a clockwise manner over a multiple of three threads.

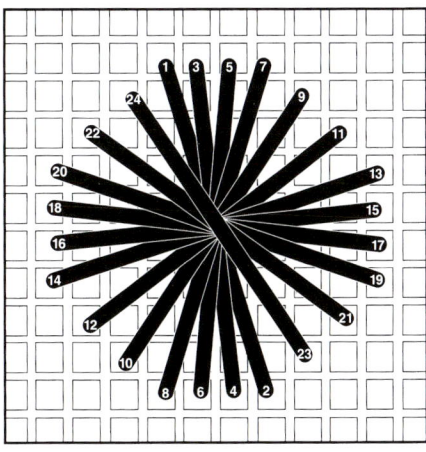

RHODES STITCH — STAR

Follow the numbers to work the outside stitches in a counterclockwise direction. Work the Cross Stitch at the center last.

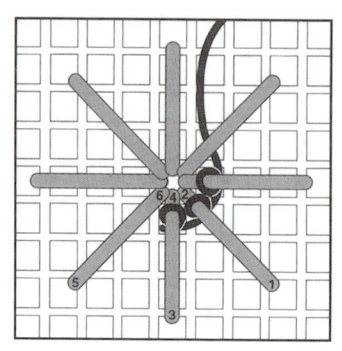

A

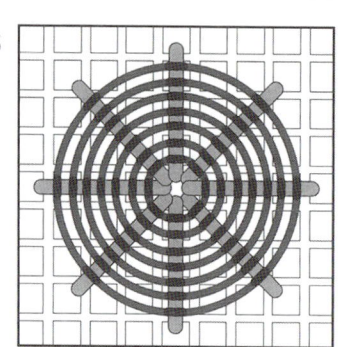

B

RIBBED WHEEL STITCH

Use a one-yard length of yarn to work this stitch. This stitch is formed by first stitching eight spokes into a central hole (**A**). Bring needle up near the central hole. Refer to **A** and wrap yarn around each spoke once before going under the next spoke. Continue working in the same direction to completely cover each spoke (**B**). Go down near a spoke end to finish.

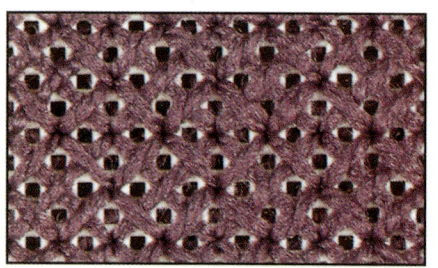
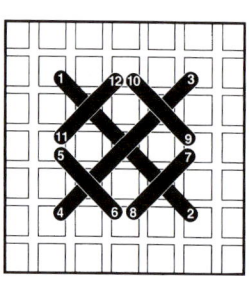

RICE STITCH

This decorative stitch is formed by first working a large Cross Stitch over four threads, then working a stitch over each leg of the Cross Stitch. A second color may be used for the stitch over each leg.

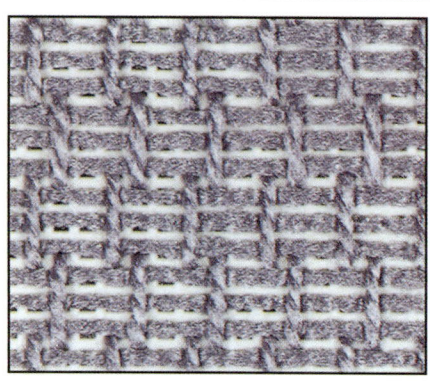
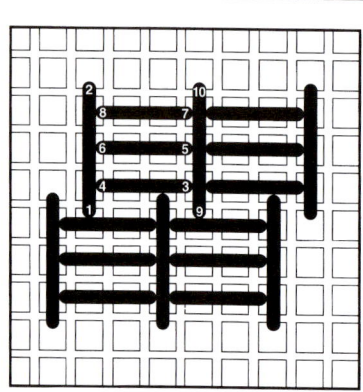

ROMAN STITCH

This stitch is a combination of straight stitches.

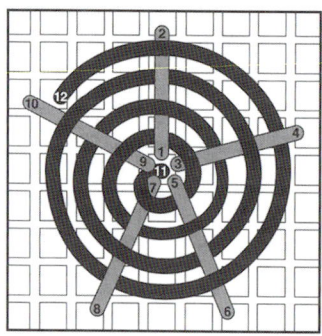

ROSE STITCH

Use a 1½-yard length of yarn to work this stitch. Work five spokes into the same central hole. Bring needle up in the central hole. Weave yarn over and under spokes, keeping tension slightly loose. Continue weaving until spokes are fully covered. Pull yarn slightly to "puff" rose.

SCOTCH STITCH — BASIC
This series of slanted stitches, worked over three or more threads, forms squares.

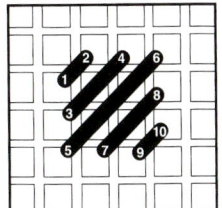 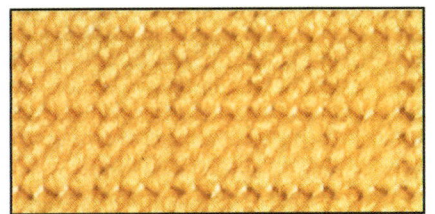

SCOTCH STITCH — ALTERNATING
In this variation of the Scotch Stitch, the stitches in each square slant in the opposite direction from the stitches in the previously stitched square.

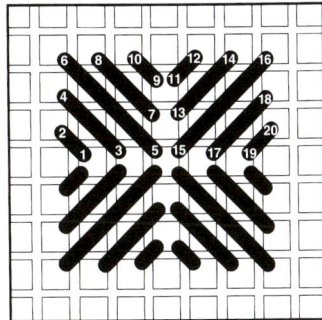 

SCOTCH STITCH — BOXED
A border of Tent Stitches is worked around each Scotch Stitch.

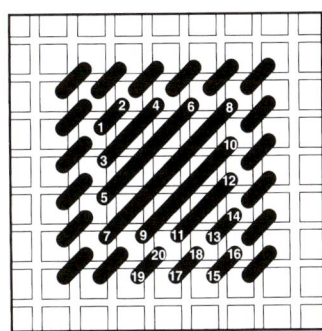 

SCOTCH STITCH — CHECKED
Scotch Stitch squares alternate with squares of nine Tent Stitches to form this pattern.

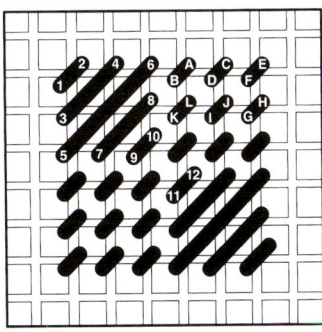 

SCOTCH STITCH — DOTTED
In this pattern, the long center stitch of each square is replaced with three Tent Stitches.

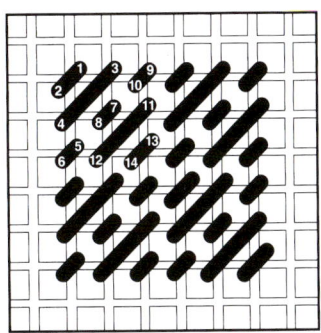 

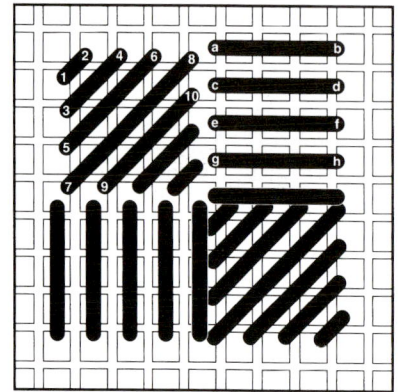

SCOTCH STITCH — PATTERNED
In this pattern, Scotch Stitches alternate with straight Gobelin Stitches to form a checkerboard pattern. Make sure to work the Gobelin Stitches over the ends of the Scotch Stitches.

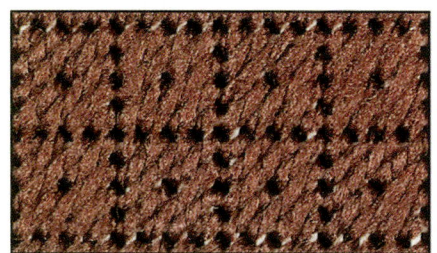
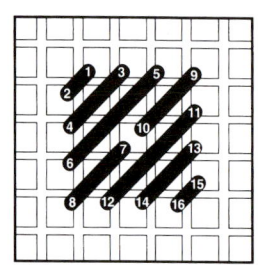

SCOTCH STITCH — VARIATION
This stitch is a Scotch Stitch with a dimple in the center.

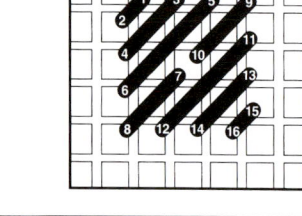
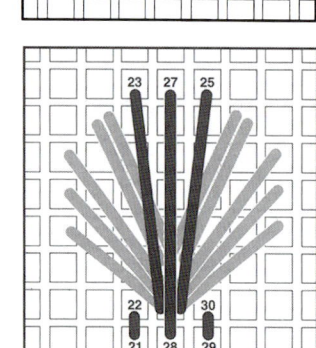

SEA SHELL STITCH
This large stitch makes a nice border. It is composed of long, slanting Gobelin Stitches. Complete the stitches in **A**; then, add the stitches in **B** for each individual Sea Shell Stitch.

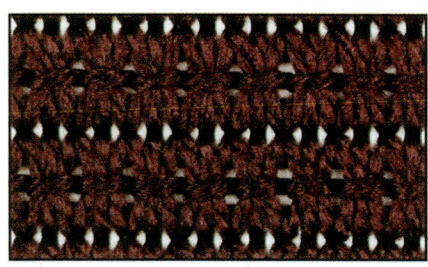
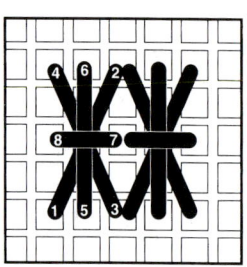

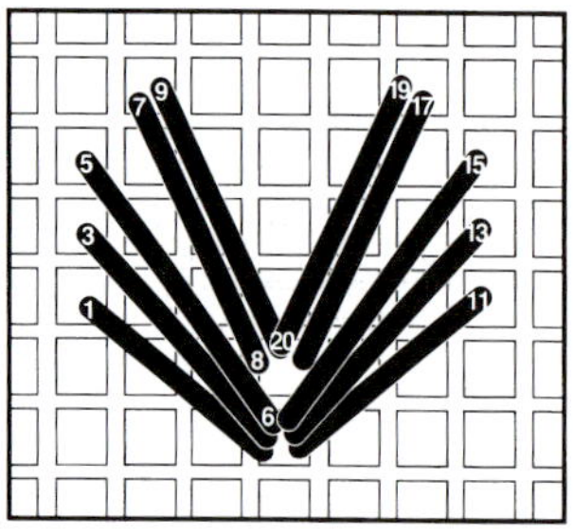

SHEAF STITCH
This stitch is composed of three upright stitches drawn together in the middle by a horizontal tie-down stitch. Complete each stitch before going on to the next.

SHELL STITCH

This stitch is composed of three upright stitches drawn together in the middle by a horizontal tie-down stitch. After working all Shell Stitches, work straight stitches.

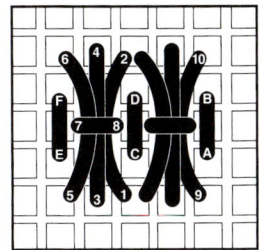 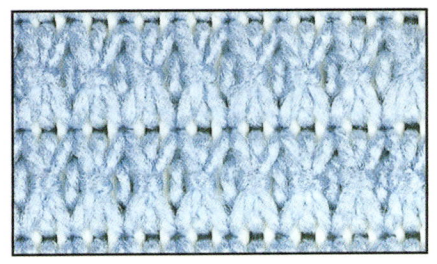

SMOOTH SPIDER WEB STITCH

This decorative stitch is made by first stitching eight spokes into a central hole, using a 1½-yard piece of yarn (**A**). Come up through a hole next to the central hole. Weave over two spokes and back under one spoke until all spokes are covered (**B**).

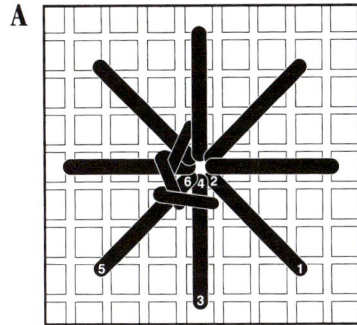
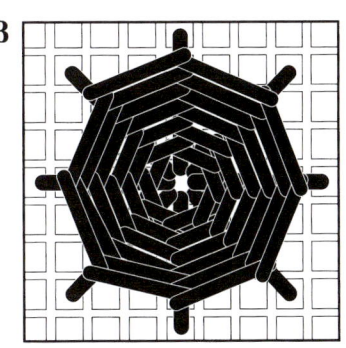
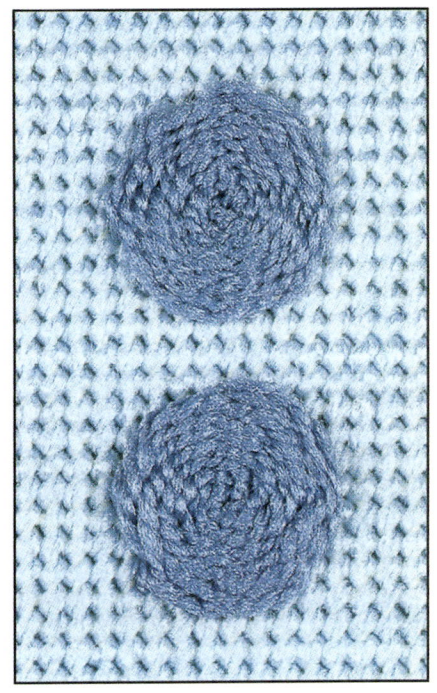

STEM STITCH — BASIC

The Stem Stitch is a series of slanted stitches worked vertically with each row changing direction.

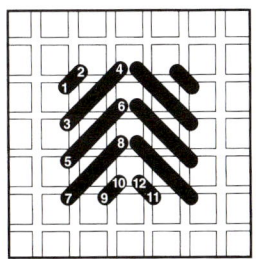 

STEM STITCH — VARIATION

This variation is a series of slanted stitches worked vertically with each row changing direction. A row of Backstitches is worked between the slanted stitches.

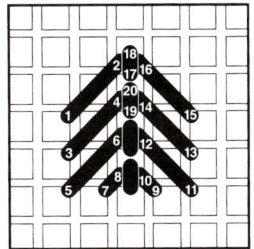 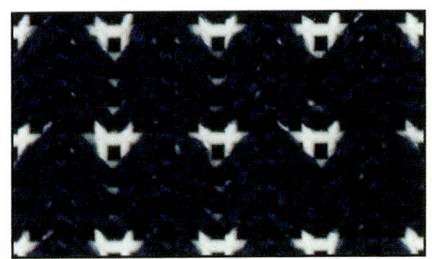

25

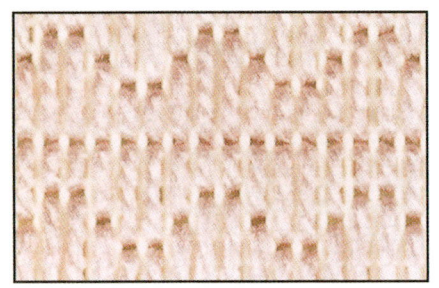 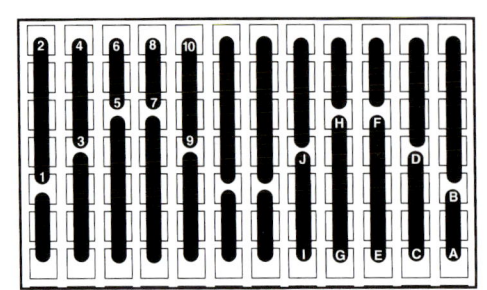

SUTHERLAND STITCH — BASIC
This stitch is formed by working straight stitches that form a wavy pattern.

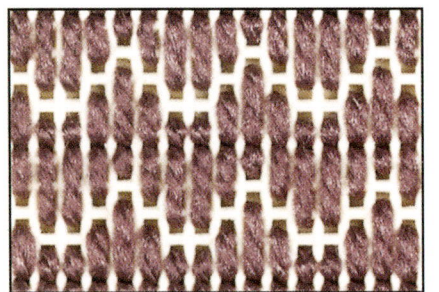 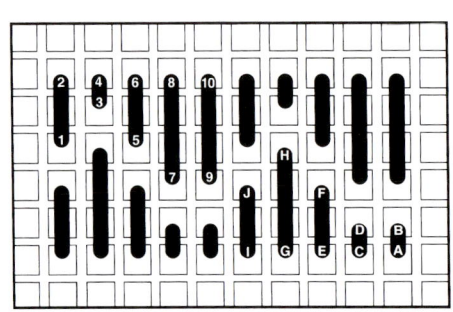

SUTHERLAND STITCH — VARIATION
This variation of the Sutherland Stitch is formed by leaving an empty thread between the straight stitches that form a wavy pattern. This stitch would work well on colored plastic canvas.

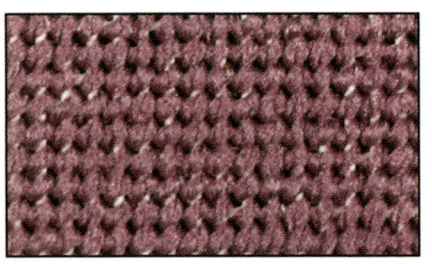 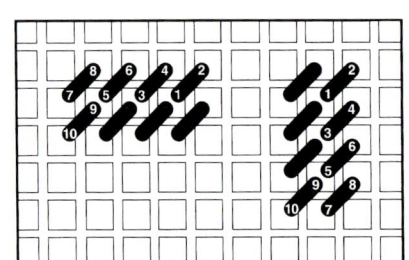

TENT STITCH — BASIC
This stitch is worked in horizontal or vertical rows over one intersection. Tent Stitches slant from lower left to upper right.

 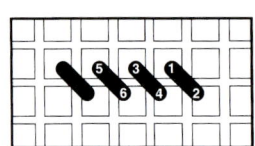

TENT STITCH — REVERSED
This stitch is worked in horizontal or vertical rows over one intersection. Reversed Tent Stitches slant from upper left to lower right.

 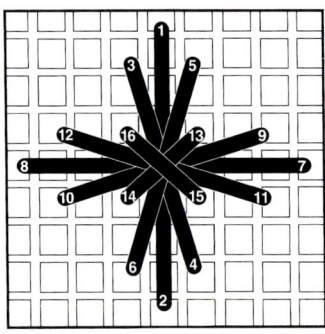

TIED WINDMILL STITCH
The top stitch of the cross may vary, but all stitches on a stitched piece should be made in the same direction.

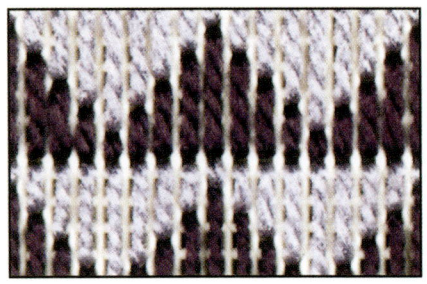 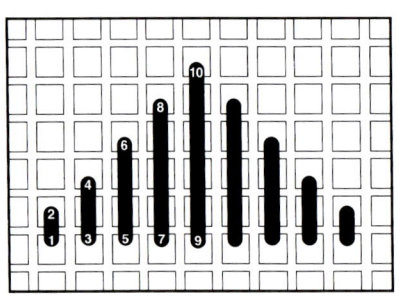

TRIANGLE STITCH
A series of straight stitches form a triangle. The size of the triangle may vary. The triangle may be inverted to create an interlocking pattern.

TURKEY LOOP STITCH
To work this locked-loop stitch, bring needle up through hole and back down through same hole, forming a loop on top of the canvas. A locking stitch is then made across the thread directly below or to either side of the loop.

 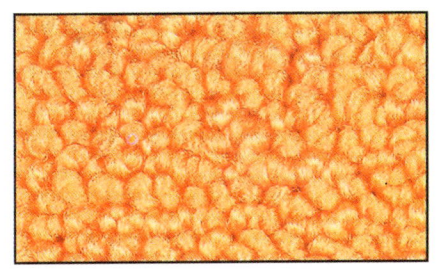

VICTORIAN STEP STITCH
The pattern is a series of straight stitches which form a stair-step design.

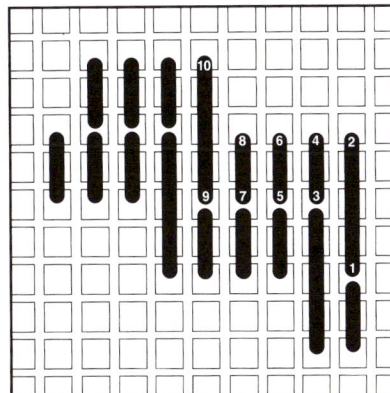 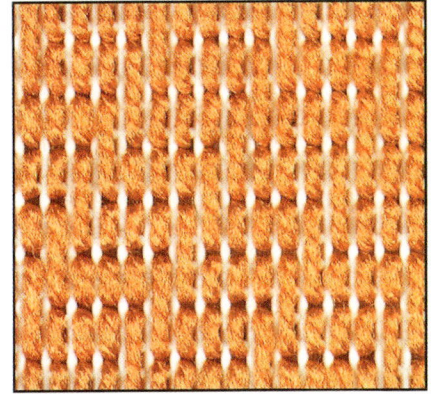

WAFFLE STITCH
This square stitch has a woven look and may be worked over any number of threads.

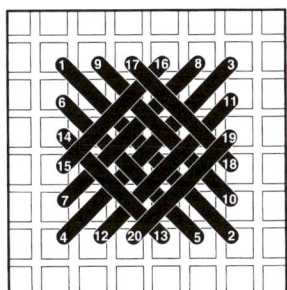 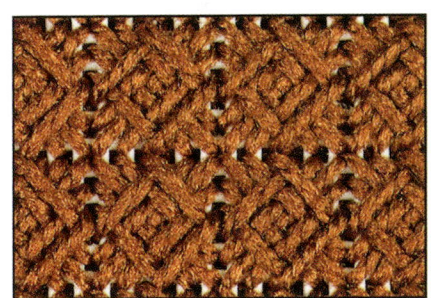

WOVEN PLAIT STITCH
This stitch looks like the Square Herringbone Stitch but is worked in diagonal rows.

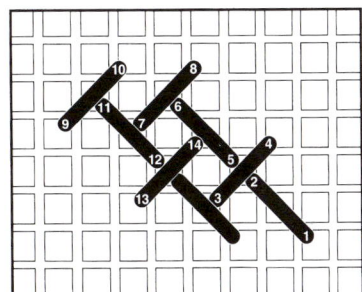 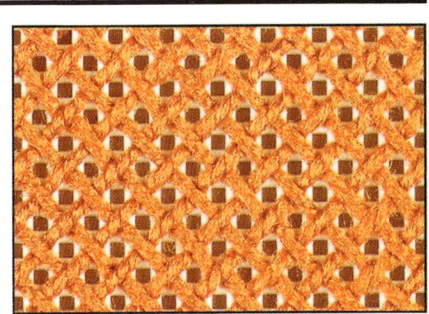

WOVEN STITCH
When working the Woven Stitch, the first row is worked from left to right and the second row from right to left.

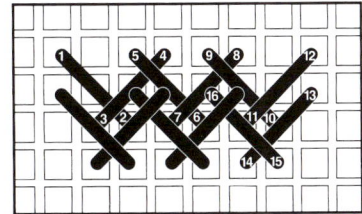 

SAMPLE PROJECTS

The projects on the next 10 pages feature many of the stitches from the Stitch Dictionary. By seeing how different stitches can be used together and seeing the role that color choice plays in the completed project, we hope you will be inspired to design your own plastic canvas creations. Most of plastic canvas pieces are cut in standard sizes so that you may also use these pieces as templates for future projects.

TISSUE BOX COVER

Size: 4½"w x 5¾"h x 4½"d
Fits a 4¼"w x 5¼"h x 4¼"d boutique tissue box.
Supplies: Worsted weight or plastic canvas yarn in colors of your choice, one 10½" x 13½" sheet of 7 mesh plastic canvas, and #16 tapestry needle.
Instructions:
1. Follow charts to cut pieces. Stitch pieces as charted or with stitches of your choice. We've labeled each type of stitch we used.
2. Join Sides along long edges; join Top to Sides. Cover bottom unworked edges. We used Overcast Stitch and Braided Cross Stitch to join our Tissue Box Covers and to cover the bottom unworked edges.

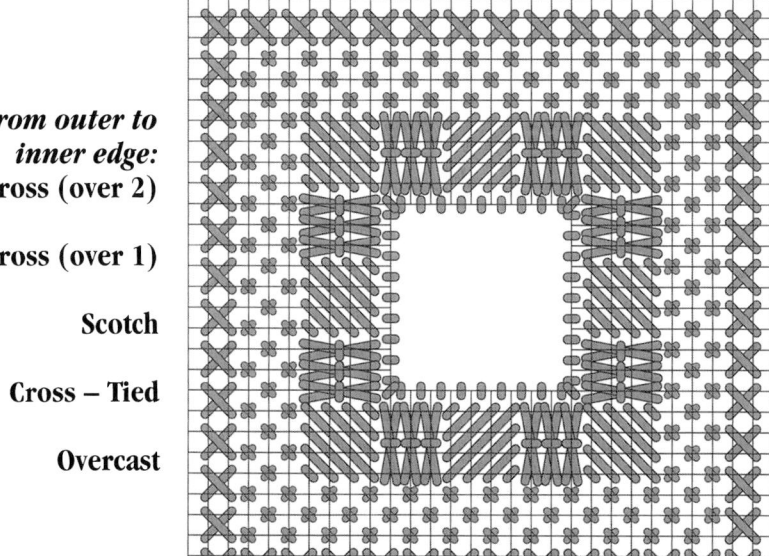

Top (30 x 30 threads)

From outer to inner edge:
Cross (over 2)
Cross (over 1)
Scotch
Cross – Tied
Overcast

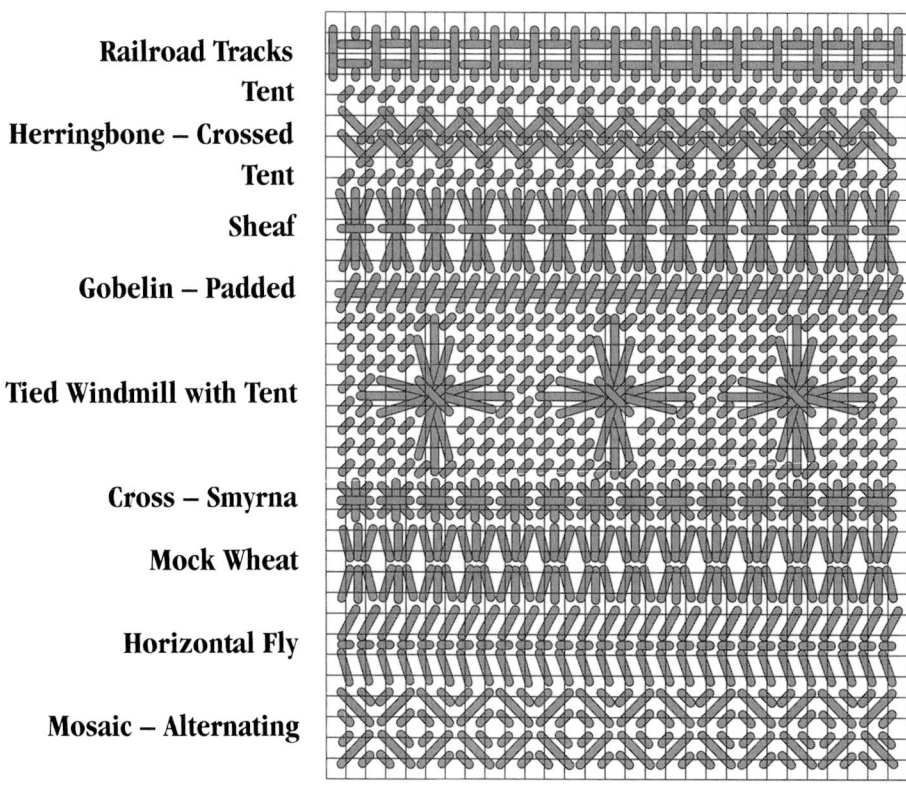

Side (30 x 38 threads) (stitch 4)

Railroad Tracks
Tent
Herringbone – Crossed
Tent
Sheaf
Gobelin – Padded

Tied Windmill with Tent

Cross – Smyrna
Mock Wheat

Horizontal Fly

Mosaic – Alternating

DOORSTOP

Size: 8½"w x 4¼"h x 2½"d

This Doorstop is designed to fit a brick 7½"w x 3½"h x 2⅛"d. If your brick is smaller, the Doorstop may be padded with tissue paper.

Supplies: Worsted weight or plastic canvas yarn in colors of your choice, two 10½" x 13½" sheets of 7 mesh plastic canvas, #16 tapestry needle, and plastic wrap.

Instructions:

1. Follow charts to cut pieces. Stitch pieces as charted or with stitches of your choice. We've labeled each type of stitch we used.
2. Join Front, Back, and Long Sides along long edges; join one Short Side to Front, Back, and Long Sides. We used Overcast Stitch to join our Doorstop.
3. Wrap brick in plastic wrap. Insert brick and join remaining Short Side to Front, Back, and Long Sides.

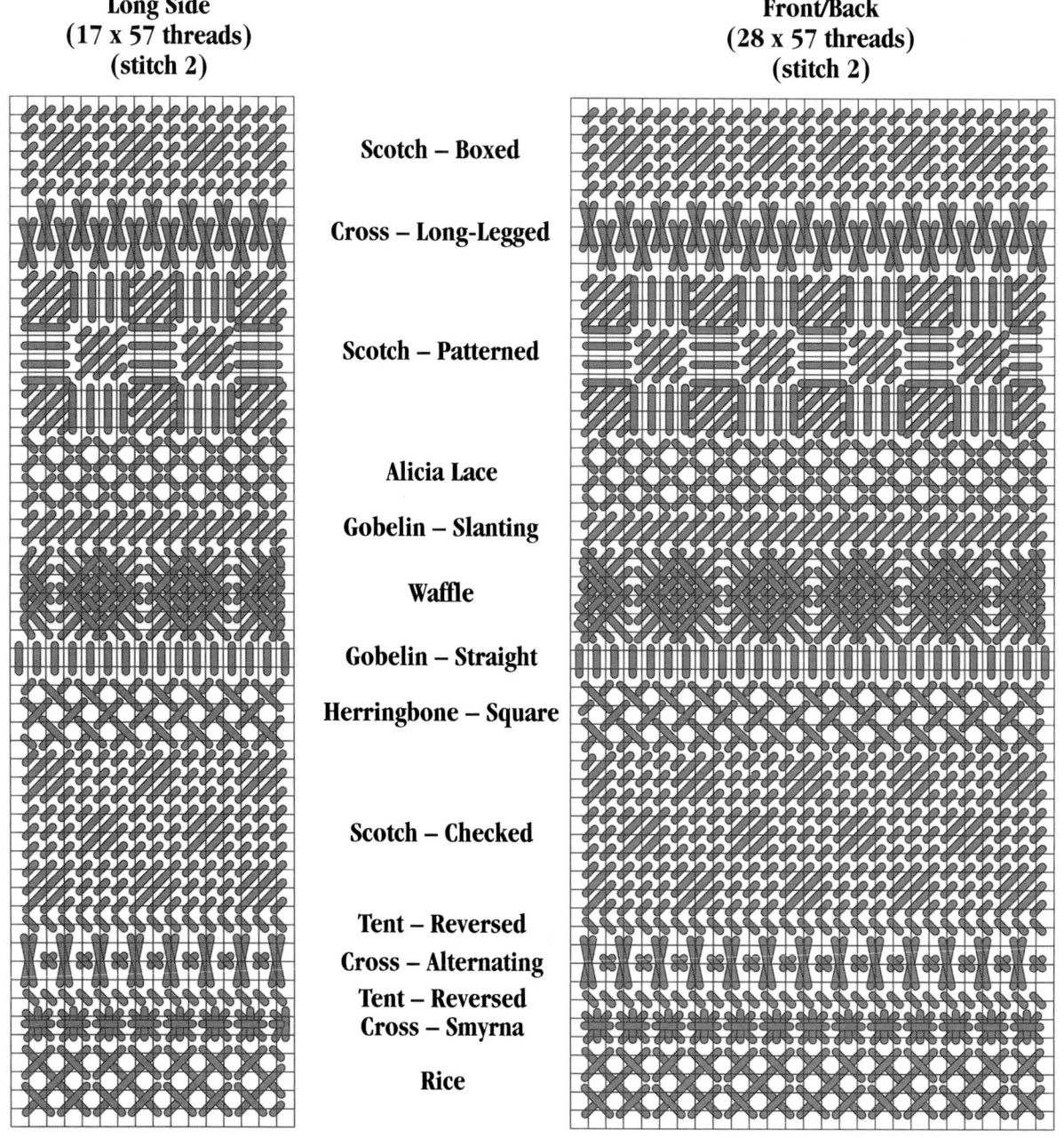

Long Side (17 x 57 threads) (stitch 2)

Front/Back (28 x 57 threads) (stitch 2)

Scotch – Boxed
Cross – Long-Legged
Scotch – Patterned
Alicia Lace
Gobelin – Slanting
Waffle
Gobelin – Straight
Herringbone – Square
Scotch – Checked
Tent – Reversed
Cross – Alternating
Tent – Reversed
Cross – Smyrna
Rice

Short Side
(28 x 17 threads)
(stitch 2)

From outer edge to center:
Triangle

Gobelin – Straight

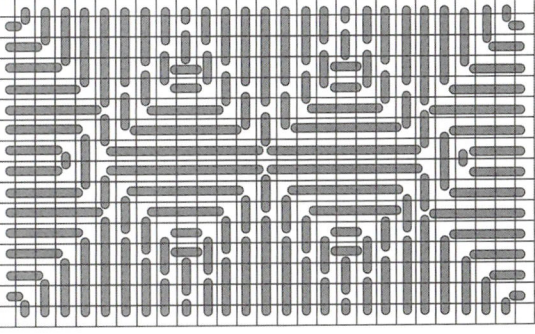

31

BELLPULL SAMPLER

Size: 6½"w x 24"h (excluding fringe)

Supplies: Worsted weight or plastic canvas yarn in colors of your choice, one 13½" x 22" sheet of 7 mesh plastic canvas, #16 tapestry needle, 9" long pre-finished wooden dowel with decorative ends, and craft glue.

Instructions:

1. Cut one piece of canvas 43 x 151 threads for Bellpull. Beginning with Stitching Section #1, follow charts to stitch Bellpull as charted or with stitches of your choice. We've labeled each row with the stitches we used. Use Overcast Stitch to cover all unworked edges of Bellpull.

2. Follow chart to cut Hanging Tabs. Stitch as charted or with stitches of your choice. Use Overcast Stitch to cover long unworked edges of Hanging Tabs.

3. Join short edges of Hanging Tabs to Bellpull along top edge. We used Overcast Stitch to join our Hanging Tabs to the Bellpull. Trim Fringe.

Bellpull Sampler — Stitching Section #1
Bellpull Sampler is one piece of canvas (43 x 151 threads).

Tent
Cross – Long-Legged
Rhodes – Star with Triangle
Herringbone – Crossed
Shell
Stem
Cross – Upright
Tent
Barred Square with Cross (over 2)
Tent
Cross – Tied Double
Byzantine
Cross (over 1)
Cross (over 2)
Cross (over 1)
Tent, Cross – Long-Legged, and Ribbed Wheel

Continued on pg. 34.

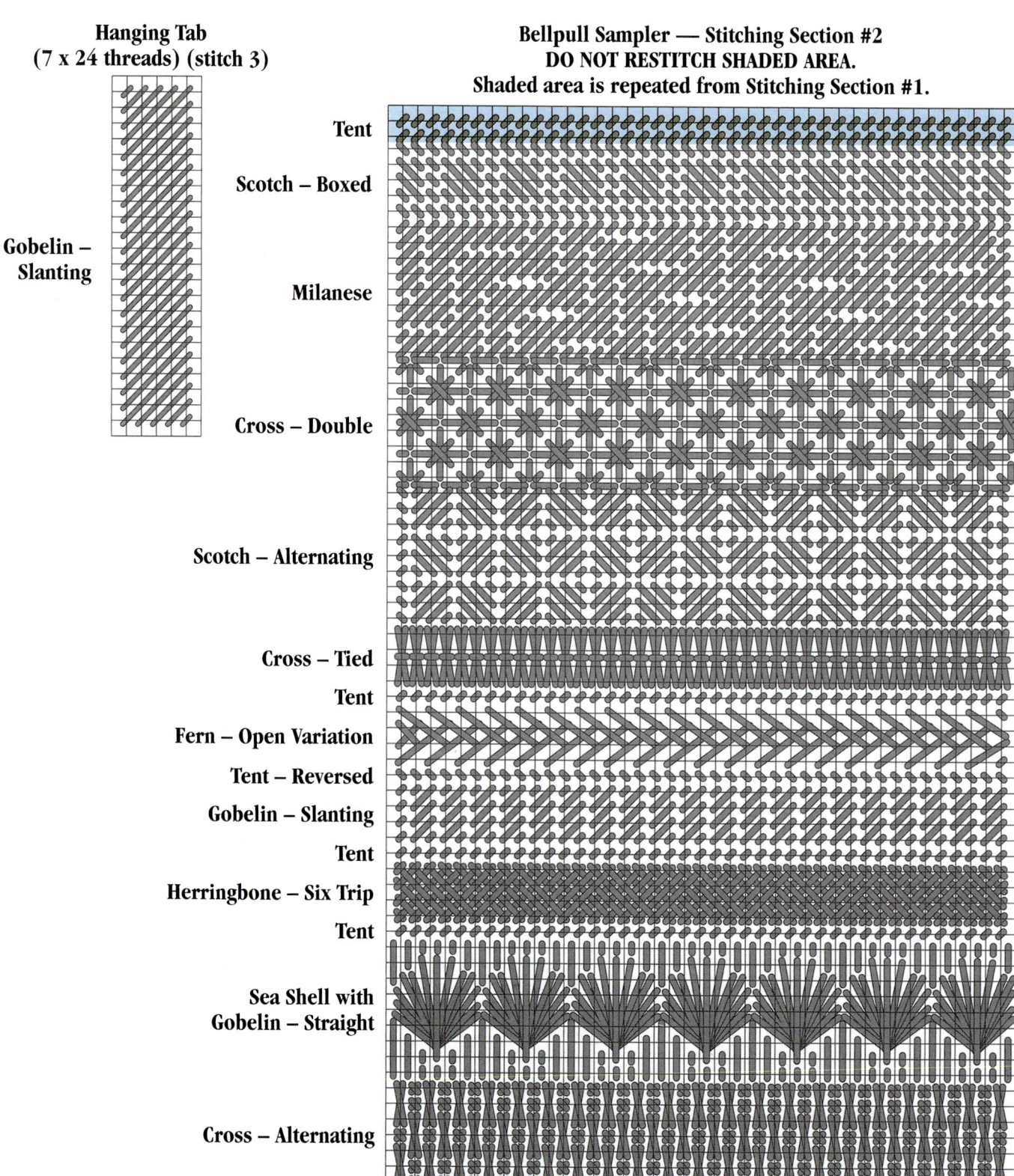

EYEGLASS CASE

Size: 3¾"w x 7¼"h
Supplies: Worsted weight or plastic canvas yarn in colors of your choice, one 10½" x 13½" sheet of 7 mesh plastic canvas, #16 tapestry needle, felt, and craft glue.

Instructions:
1. Follow chart to cut pieces. Stitch pieces as charted or with stitches of your choice. We've labeled each type of stitch we used.
2. For lining, cut two pieces of felt slightly smaller than Front and Back. Glue felt to wrong side of Front and Back.
3. Join Front to Back along unworked edges. We used Overcast Stitch to join our Eyeglass Case.

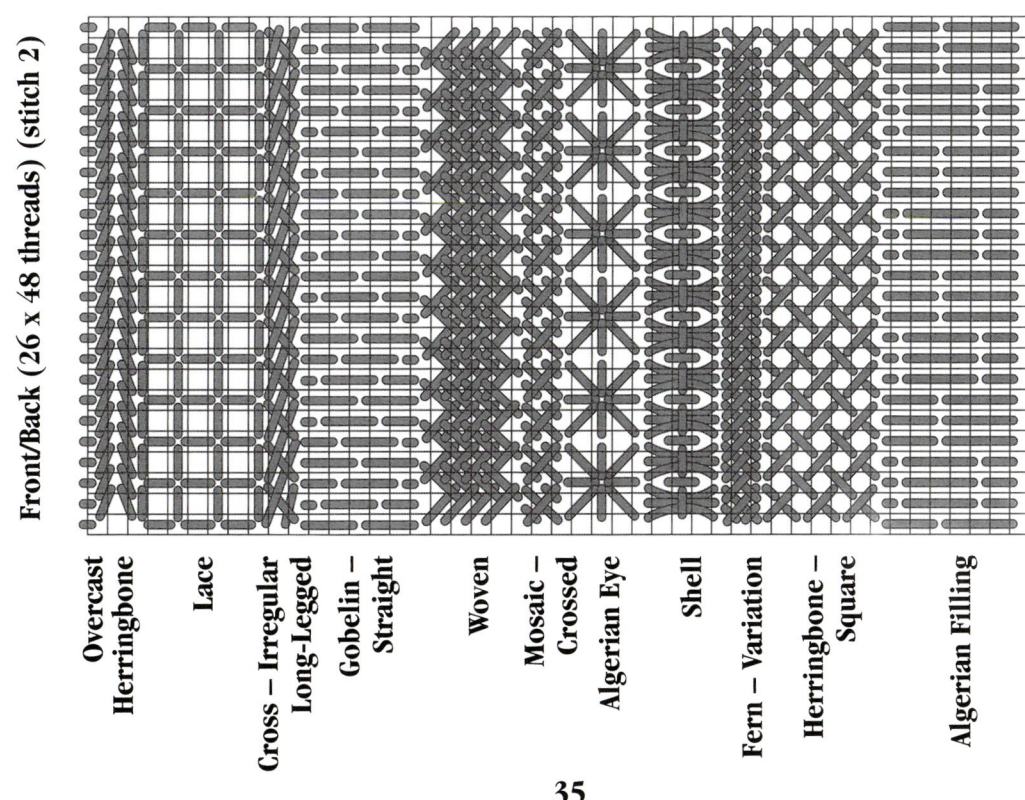

Front/Back (26 x 48 threads) (stitch 2)

Overcast • Herringbone • Lace • Cross – Irregular Long-Legged • Gobelin – Straight • Woven • Mosaic – Crossed • Algerian Eye • Shell • Fern – Variation • Herringbone – Square • Algerian Filling

COASTERS

Size: 3¾"w x 3¾"h each
Supplies: Worsted weight or plastic canvas yarn in colors of your choice, one 10½" x 13½" sheet of 7 mesh plastic canvas, and #16 tapestry needle. If backing is desired, you will also need cork or felt and craft glue.

Instructions:
1. Follow charts to cut Coasters. Stitch as charted or with stitches of your choice. We've labeled each type of stitch we used.
2. Use desired color yarn to cover edges. We used Overcast Stitch to cover the edges of our Coasters.
3. If backing is desired, cut a piece of cork or felt slightly smaller than each Coaster. Glue backing to wrong side of each Coaster.

Coaster
(26 x 26 threads)

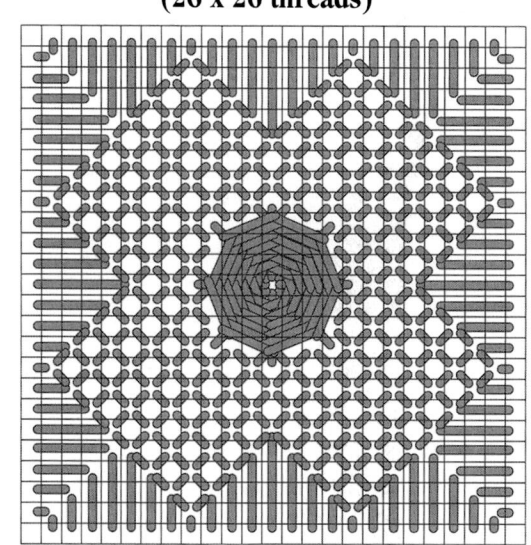

From outer edge to center:
Gobelin – Straight

Alicia Lace

Smooth Spider Web

Coaster
(26 x 26 threads)

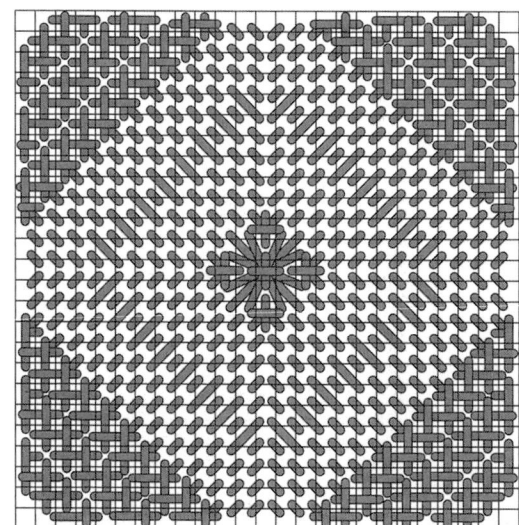

From outer edge to center:
Cross – Diagonal Upright

Tent and Tent – Reversed

Mosaic – Diagonal

Leviathan – Double Variation

Coaster
(26 x 26 threads)

Coaster
(26 x 26 threads)

From outer edge to center:
Milanese

Backstitch – General Coverage

Waffle

From outer edge to center:
Byzantine – Irregular

Cross (over 1)

Tent and Tent – Reversed

Rhodes – Diamond

STITCH SPECIFICS

This dictionary includes our best efforts to illustrate the wide variety of stitches available to you along with some hints for successful plastic canvas stitching. Use these stitches and our suggestions to create your own designs.

TYPES OF STITCHES

General Coverage Stitches. These stitches are used to cover large areas of canvas. Tent, Gobelin, and Mosaic Stitches are some of the typical general coverage stitches.

Accent Stitches. These stitches are used to provide detail and decorations. They include such stitches as French Knots, Backstitches, and the more complex, Rhodes Stitches.

Joining Stitches. These stitches, the most popular being the Overcast Stitch, are used to join pieces of canvas.

COMPENSATING STITCHES

When using many of the stitches in this dictionary, you should be aware that you may not always be able to begin or complete the stitch patterns at all edges of the canvas. In that case, you must also use small stitches called compensating stitches to fill in your canvas (black stitches shown in **Fig. 1**).

Fig. 1

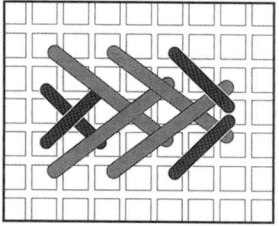

STITCH PLACEMENT

This dictionary illustrates the stitches used in the typical horizontal, vertical, or diagonal manner and over a particular number of threads. When experimenting with your designs, don't let your imagination be stifled by our suggestions. Be creative with stitch placement. Try changing the direction of the stitches or using mirror images to achieve your desired effect. You may also change the number of threads covered by a stitch to enhance your patterns.

PLASTIC CANVAS POINTERS

SELECTING CANVAS

Mesh Size. The main difference between types of plastic canvas is the mesh size. Mesh size refers to the number of holes in one inch of canvas. Seven mesh is the most popular size of canvas used in projects.

5 mesh = 5 holes per inch
7 mesh = 7 holes per inch
10 mesh = 10 holes per inch
14 mesh = 14 holes per inch

Canvas Colors. Most projects are stitched on clear canvas, but canvas is also available in a wide range of colors. Try using an open stitch pattern on colored canvas if you don't want to stitch the entire background. The color of the canvas then becomes a part of your design.

Canvas Pliability. Some canvas is firm and rigid while other canvas is more soft and pliable. The type of canvas you will need is based on how the project will be used. Choose a firm canvas if your project needs support or a softer canvas when little support is desired or for ease in bending.

Amount of Canvas. When buying canvas, remember that several different manufacturers produce plastic canvas; therefore, there are often slight variations in canvas. Because of these variations, try to buy enough canvas for your entire project at the same time and from the same manufacturer. As a general rule, it is always better to buy too much canvas and use the leftovers for practice or small projects.

SELECTING NEEDLES

A blunt needle called a tapestry needle is used for stitching on plastic canvas. Tapestry needles are sized by numbers; the higher the number, the smaller the needle. Generally, the correct size needle to use depends on the canvas mesh size (see table below). You may wish to use a smaller needle depending on the yarn thickness or number of plies of yarn or strands of embroidery floss.

Mesh	Needle
5	#16
7	#16
10	#20
14	#24

SELECTING YARN

Colors. Color is the easiest way to personalize a project and make it truly unique. We have not suggested colors in this dictionary. Most leaflets include color keys which tell you the color of yarn used to stitch the photography models. It's a good idea to think of color keys as "suggested colors." When brand names and color numbers are listed in color keys, use them as a guide when choosing colors.

Dye Lot Variations. It is important to buy all of the yarn you need to complete your project from the same dye lot. Although variations in color may be slight when yarns from two different dye lots are held together, the variation is usually apparent on a stitched piece.

Uses of Project. When choosing yarn for your project, consider how the project will be used. If your finished piece will receive a great deal of wear, choose a sturdy, washable yarn, such as acrylic or nylon yarn. If your finished piece won't be handled or used frequently, you are not limited to washable yarns.

Amounts. A handy way to estimate yardage is to make a yarn yardage estimator. Cut a one-yard length of yarn for each different stitch used in your project. For each stitch, work as many stitches as you can with the one-yard length of yarn.

To use your yarn yardage estimator, count the number of stitches you were able to make, say 72 Tent Stitches. Now look at the chart for the project you want to make. Estimate the number of ecru Tent Stitches on the chart, say 150. Divide the estimated number of ecru Tent Stitches by the actual number stitched with a yard of yarn. One hundred fifty divided by 72 is a bit more than two. So you will need slightly more than two yards of ecru yarn to make your project. Repeat this for all stitches and yarn colors. To allow for repairs and practice stitches, purchase extra yardage of each color.

TYPES OF YARN AND THREADS

Worsted Weight Yarn – Worsted weight yarn is the most popular yarn used for 7 mesh plastic canvas because one strand covers the canvas well. It works equally well on 5 mesh when you use two strands. This yarn may be found in acrylic, wool, wool blends, and a variety of other fiber contents. Acrylic yarn is a favorite because it is reasonably priced and comes in a wide variety of colors. Most brands of worsted weight yarn have four plies that are twisted together to form one strand.

Plastic Canvas Yarn – Plastic canvas yarn is designed for use on 5 and 7 mesh plastic canvas. This yarn is sturdy and provides good coverage with one strand on 7 mesh and two strands on 5 mesh. It is available in acrylic, nylon, and a variety of other fiber contents. This yarn does not usually separate easily.

Sport Weight Yarn – Sport weight yarn works nicely on 10 mesh canvas. This yarn has three or four thin plies that are twisted together to form one strand. Like worsted weight yarn, sport weight yarn comes in a variety of fiber contents. The color selection in sport weight yarn is more limited than in other types of yarns. If you can't find sport weight yarn in the color needed, worsted weight yarn may be substituted; simply remove one ply of the yarn and stitch with the remaining three plies.

Tapestry Yarn – This thin, wool yarn is available in a wider variety of colors than other yarns and may be used when several shades of the same color are desired. Tapestry yarn is ideal for working on 10 mesh canvas. However, it is a more expensive yarn and requires two strands to cover 7 mesh canvas. Projects made with tapestry yarn cannot be washed.

Persian Wool – This is a wool yarn that is made up of three loosely twisted plies. The plies should be separated and realigned before you thread your needle. Like tapestry yarn, Persian wool has more shades of each color from which to choose. It can be used on any mesh size canvas. Because of the wool content, you cannot wash projects made with Persian wool.

Pearl Cotton – Sometimes #3 pearl cotton is used on plastic canvas to give it a dressy, lacy look. It is not meant to cover 7 mesh canvas completely, but to enhance it. Pearl cotton works well on 10 and 14 mesh canvas when you want your needlework to have a satiny sheen.

Embroidery Floss – Embroidery floss is made up of six strands. For smooth coverage when using embroidery floss, separate and realign the strands of floss before threading your needle. Twelve strands of floss may be used for covering 10 mesh canvas. Use six strands to cover 14 mesh canvas. Embroidery floss can also be used to add details on 7 mesh canvas by using six strands of floss.

Metallic Yarn – This flat yarn is soft, flexible, and durable. Metallic yarn can be used to add decorative details to a project or for general coverage. It is available in different sizes for use with various mesh sizes. Use 18" or shorter lengths of metallic yarn for easier stitching and to avoid fraying. Since metallic yarn is flat instead of round like other yarns and metallic braids, care must be used to make sure the yarn lies flat when stitched on the canvas.

Metallic Braid – Metallic braid is available in a variety of sizes and may be used to add finishing details to a project or for general coverage. Using 18" or shorter lengths of metallic braid will make stitching easier and avoid excessive wear.

WORKING WITH PLASTIC CANVAS

Counting Threads. In the sample projects in this dictionary, the lines of the canvas are referred to as threads. To cut plastic canvas pieces accurately, count **threads** (not **holes**) as shown in **Fig. 2**.

Fig. 2

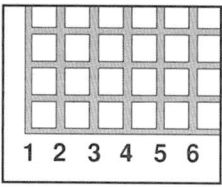

Preparing And Cutting Canvas. Before cutting, you may want to use an overhead projector pen to outline the piece on the canvas before cutting it out. Before you begin stitching, remove all markings with a damp paper towel.

Using a good pair of household scissors, cut out your pieces. Cut as close to the threads as possible. A craft knife is helpful for cutting small areas and for removing the "nubs" or "pickets" that could snag your yarn. Protect your work surface when using a craft knife.

STITCHING THE DESIGN

Threading Your Needle. Several brands of yarn-size needle threaders are available at your local craft store. Here are a couple of methods that may make threading your needle easier without a purchased threader.

Folded Yarn Method – First, sharply fold the end of yarn over your needle; then, remove needle. Keeping the fold sharp, push the needle onto the folded yarn (**Fig. 3**).

Fig. 3

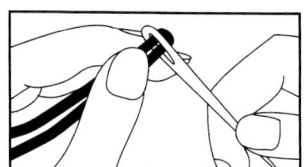

Thread Method – Fold a 6" piece of sewing thread in half, forming a loop. Insert loop of thread through the eye of your needle (**Fig. 4**). Insert yarn through the loop and pull the thread back through your needle, pulling yarn through at the same time.

Fig. 4

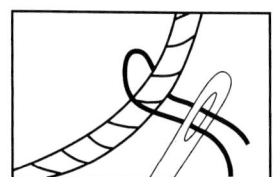

Securing the First Stitch. Don't knot the end of your yarn before you begin stitching. Instead, begin each length of yarn by coming up from the wrong side of the canvas and leaving a 1" - 2" tail on the wrong side. Hold this tail against the canvas and work the first few stitches over the tail. Trim off any excess.

Length of Yarn. It is best to begin stitching with a piece of yarn that is approximately one-yard long. However, when working large areas of the same color, you may want to begin with a longer length of yarn to reduce the number of yarn ends and keep the back of your project looking neat.

Using Even Tension. Keep your stitching tension consistent, with each stitch lying flat and even on the canvas.

Keeping Stitches Smooth. Most stitches tend to twist the yarn. Drop your needle and let the yarn untwist every few stitches or whenever needed.

Ending Your Stitches. After you've completed all of the stitches of one color in an area, end your stitching by running your needle under several stitches on the back of the stitched piece.

JOINING PIECES

Straight Edges. To join two pieces of canvas, place one piece on top of the other with right or wrong sides together. Make sure the edges being joined are even; then, stitch the pieces together through all layers.

Uneven Edges. Sometimes you'll have to join a diagonal edge to a straight edge. The holes of the two pieces will not line up exactly. Just keep the pieces even and stitch through holes as many times as necessary to completely cover the canvas.

Tacking. To tack pieces, run your needle under the backs of some stitches on one stitched piece to secure the yarn. Then run your needle through the canvas or under the stitches on the piece to be tacked in place. The idea is to securely attach your pieces without your tacking stitches showing.

WASHING YOUR PROJECT

Since plastic canvas is washable, you may hand wash projects in warm water with a mild detergent if you stitched your entire project with washable yarn. When the piece is dry, trim the fuzz from your project with a small pair of sharp scissors or a sweater shaver. Plastic canvas can't be professionally dry-cleaned or put in a clothes dryer.

Some cover models made by Connie McGaughey.

We have made every effort to ensure that these instructions are accurate and complete. We cannot, however, be responsible for human error, typographical mistakes, or variations in individual work.